Designing Innovative High Schools

Implementation of the Opportunity by Design Initiative After Two Years

Elizabeth D. Steiner, Laura S. Hamilton,
Laura Stelitano, and Mollie Rudnick

RAND
CORPORATION

Library of Congress Cataloging-in-Publication Data is available for this publication.
ISBN: 978-0-8330-9939-6

Published by the RAND Corporation, Santa Monica, Calif.
© Copyright 2017 RAND Corporation
RAND® is a registered trademark.

PHOTO CREDITS | Cover: asiseeit/E+/Getty Images; page xiii: FatCamera/Vetta/Getty Images; page 9, 15, 16, 22: asiseeit/E+/Getty Images; page 26: monkeybusinessimages/iStock/Getty Images Plus; page 28: Rawpixel/ iStock/Getty Images Plus; page 30: kali9/E+/Getty Images; page 32: FatCamera/E+/Getty Images Plus; page 34: fstop123/E+/Getty Images; page 37: asiseeit/E+/Getty Images; page 40: jacoblund/iStock/Getty Images Plus; page 46: asiseeit/E+/Getty Images; page 52: kali9/E+/Getty Images

 EDUCATION

RR-2005-CCNY
September 2017
Prepared for the Carnegie Corporation of New York

Preface

The Carnegie Corporation of New York's (CCNY's) Opportunity by Design (ObD) initiative provides support for new, small high schools of choice in several districts across the United States to adopt a set of design principles intended to ensure that students are prepared for college and careers. CCNY engaged the RAND Corporation in 2014 to conduct a comprehensive, formative, and summative evaluation of ObD. This report summarizes the methods and findings from the second year of this five-year evaluation and is intended to provide formative feedback related to the implementation of ObD. This research is being conducted within RAND Education, a unit of the RAND Corporation, under a grant from CCNY.

Table of Contents

Figures

Tables

Summary

Introduction

High schools across the United States are working to prepare all students with the academic, social, and emotional skills needed to be successful in postsecondary education and careers. Several reform strategies enacted in high schools over the past few decades have shown promising results; these include the creation of small learning communities, innovations in career and technical education, and increased access to rigorous coursework. Despite these efforts, however, levels of student achievement have remained largely stagnant over the past few decades, and sizable gaps in academic achievement and graduation rates among socioeconomic and racial/ethnic groups persist (National Assessment of Educational Progress, undated; National Center for Education Statistics, 2016). Moreover, employers have expressed concerns about inadequate development of inter- and intrapersonal skills, such as teamwork and responsibility, that are essential for effective job performance (*Are They Really Ready to Work? Employers' Perspectives on the Basic*

Knowledge and Applied Skills of New Entrants to the 21st Century U.S. Workforce, 2006). High schools continue to face pressure to improve outcomes for all students across a variety of academic and nonacademic dimensions.

To address this challenge, the Carnegie Corporation of New York (CCNY) founded the Opportunity by Design (ObD) initiative in 2013 to support the design and launch of a network of small high schools of choice that focus on ten design principles (see Figure S.1). The design principles, if fully implemented, should result in a school that looks different from a traditional high school. The initiative provided funding and technical support to the schools during a design year prior to opening the school and for two years of implementation—with the expectation that the schools would design their models to be self-sustaining on public funds. The first ObD schools opened in fall 2014, and the last will open in fall 2017. Through the ObD initiative, CCNY, along with the capacity-building

---

FIGURE S.1 ObD Design Principles

A high-performing high school . . .

1. has a clear mission and coherent culture
2. prioritizes mastery of rigorous standards aligned to college and career readiness
3. personalizes student learning to meet student needs
4. maintains an effective human capital strategy aligned with school model and priorities
5. develops and deploys collective strengths
6. remains porous and connected
7. integrates positive youth development to optimize student engagement and effort
8. empowers and supports students through key transitions into and beyond high school
9. manages school operations efficiently and effectively
10. continuously improves its operations and model (CCNY, 2013).

organization Springpoint: Partners in School Design, supports the participating districts in using innovative school design to improve student outcomes and ultimately enable broader district reforms.

In email correspondence, CCNY (2017) described

[t]he objectives of the ObD initiative [as] threefold: 1) to develop innovative school models in high-poverty areas that meet students where they are, promote student-centered learning, and serve as proof points for the field; 2) build capacity of school districts and partners to create and support schools that embody the principles in a way that is authentic to the local context; and 3) build knowledge for the field about what it takes to design, launch, and support innovative school model[s] across a variety of contexts.

The RAND Corporation began conducting a five-year formative and summative evaluation of the ObD initiative in June 2014 when the first cohort of schools opened. This report is intended to be formative and describes findings from the first two years of implementation from two cohorts of schools: Cohort I schools opened in 2014–2015, and Cohort II schools opened in 2015–2016. (The sample consists of ten schools in total.) This report provides a look at the early implementation of the school models and the ten design principles, along with the conditions that facilitate and hinder implementation and how staffs have addressed those conditions so far.

The findings in this report are based on principal, teacher, and student surveys; interviews with teachers, principals, and district staff and with leaders at CCNY and Springpoint; student focus groups; parent focus groups in four schools; classroom observations; and a sample of artifacts (e.g., school handbooks) from each school, where relevant. To organize the report, we grouped our findings related to the ten ObD design principles into two domains: school culture and instruction, and school management and operations. We discuss comparisons across cohorts and years separately.

This report emphasizes three of the design principles—prioritizing mastery, personalizing learning, and positive youth development (PYD)—which CCNY (2017) refers to as "power principles," because CCNY believes they are foundational to the schools' models. It is important to acknowledge that mastery, personalization, and PYD have become common terms and are often used to describe a variety of strategies and instructional approaches. The box on this page

ObD Power Principles

- **Prioritizing mastery:** Students demonstrate deep understanding of clearly defined, rigorous competencies.

- **Personalizing learning:** Student learning experiences are tailored to individual learning needs and interests.

- **Positive youth development:** Students have voice in their learning and access to experiences and relationships that help them develop the skills and mindsets to succeed (CCNY, 2017).

provides the definitions that CCNY uses in the context of ObD.

We also discuss district contextual factors, implementation successes, challenges, and recommendations. It is important for readers to keep in mind that these findings are based primarily on self-reported data and that the sample sizes are small in some cases. We also recognize that the practices described in the design principles exist on a continuum and that schools across the United States have begun adopting many of these practices even when they do not explicitly espouse personalized and mastery-based approaches. The ObD schools were among the early adopters of these innovative practices, and, while we would expect to see these practices implemented to a greater extent in the ObD schools than in most schools nationally, there is not necessarily a clear distinction between what constitutes "typical" practice and what constitutes practices aligned with the design principles. Without a national comparison group, we are not able to determine whether the practices, facilitators, and challenges reported by ObD staff and students were substantively different from those used and experienced by educators and students nationally.

Moreover, as personalized and mastery-based learning approaches become more popular, it may become more difficult to discern differences between the ObD schools and schools nationally. However, despite these limitations, the formative data presented in this report allow us to provide detailed examples of the design principles in the ObD schools, develop rich descriptions of implementation facilitators and challenges, and examine similarities and differences across schools and districts.

Culture and Instruction

School missions were clear and aligned with the design principles, but few schools had mechanisms for ensuring that key aspects of the school model were regularly monitored to guarantee effective implementation. In interviews, school leaders and teachers described missions focused on social, emotional, and academic learning; preparing students for life after high school; mastery-based instruction; and working with underserved populations. Most teachers agreed that their school had a clear mission, and school staff described the mission in ways that were consistent both with other staff's descriptions and with the documented mission. Although there was agreement across schools that the missions were clear and grounded in the design principles, staff in only a few schools could clearly and consistently describe how key aspects of the school model were designed to support the mission, how alignment of the school model and mission were regularly monitored to ensure effective implementation, and how professional development (PD) helped staff implement the mission. In addition, most schools seemed to struggle with ensuring that key aspects of the model were regularly monitored to guarantee effective implementation, perhaps because most schools did not have clear mechanisms in place to monitor alignment.

Key challenges to mastery and personalization included inconsistent expectations for mastery, varying access to data systems, external pressure to advance students at a certain pace, and significant time required to create instructional materials. Tasks used to assess mastery varied in scope and quality. In interviews, teachers and school leaders reported that the definition of mastery, and the rubrics used to assess it, were not always clear and did not always set a high bar for student work. In three schools, the expectations for mastery were not always consistent, and some mastery tasks were low in rigor (e.g., worksheets, short quizzes) or had inconsistent expectations for rigor (i.e., higher-level work expected from some students but not from others). Although a majority of surveyed teachers agreed that they had access to high-quality assessment data and reported receiving various types of student achievement data at least monthly, many expressed a need for more or better data to support mastery-based instruction. Specifically, some teachers needed more-frequent data when using long-term performance tasks, largely

because there were no opportunities to gauge how students were doing as they worked on the task.

None of the ObD schools used a system for student advancement that was wholly mastery-based, and teacher and principal discretion was a factor in student advancement decisions. Many surveyed teachers said they felt pressure to move at a set pace through the curriculum, stemming from a need to prepare students for accountability assessments, limited teacher capacity to differentiate pace for all students, poor student attendance, and limited work completion. In interviews, some principals reported feeling pressure to ensure that students graduated within the expected four years, even if the data suggested additional time was warranted.

According to interviewed teachers, districts provided relatively few curriculum materials. Teachers and principals in nine of the ten schools described a lack of time to develop personalized materials as a challenge. Although some teachers said that building their own curriculum limited the extent to which students could learn asynchronously, others said they appreciated the freedom and flexibility they had in creating their own curriculum.

Online curricula facilitated some aspects of mastery-based and personalized learning, but were inadequate as a stand-alone instructional tool. According to surveyed teachers, many of the online programs they used as one way of personalizing instruction offered students access to personalized content and data on student progress and allowed students to progress at their own pace. However, some interviewed teachers admitted relying too heavily on online programs and expressed concerns about the quality of student learning experiences. Although many teachers we interviewed were concerned that the online curricula used in their schools were of low quality, utilizing online curricula seemed to be the only approach thus far that allowed students to truly progress (or focus on needed standards) at their own pace.

All schools made efforts to promote PYD and to integrate it into academic structures, but in general PYD was distinct from academics. School leaders and teachers at all ten ObD schools affirmed that they were making efforts to promote PYD—such as creating a positive school climate and opportunities for student leadership—and many interviewed staff said PYD was part of the school's mission and vision. In addition, all of the school models incorporated PYD in their mastery and personalization systems by facilitating student choice, taking student interests into account when designing lessons or projects, providing tailored supports, and emphasizing high expectations. However, in interviews, school staff described PYD as separate from academics. Staff in eight schools described student advisory periods—the primary method of promoting PYD—as a nonacademic period that focused on building community and relationships with students, tracking student progress, giving students an opportunity to provide input, and providing time for students to focus on developing socioemotional learning skills.

Staff and students reported positive school climates but noted that climate was also an area for improvement. All surveyed principals, and almost all teachers, agreed that students respected each other, respected school staff, and were motivated to achieve. Similarly, a large majority of surveyed students agreed that their opinions were respected and that at least one adult knew the student well. Across schools, interviewed teachers and school leaders agreed that climate and culture had improved over the course of the year but noted that there was room for further improvement, and staff at seven schools reported that creating a positive climate and culture was a top priority. In interviews, several principals characterized the need for improvement as foundational: Once they got the culture and climate "right," everything else would fall into place.

Most students reported that they received help with planning their high school experience, but about one-quarter were not sure whether they were on track to graduate on time. More than three-quarters of surveyed students reported that they had discussed with an adult at the school—either briefly or in depth—topics such as the classes they should take throughout high school, the classes they should take this year, the level of mastery they should achieve in each subject to be on track to graduate, and experiences they should try to get outside of school. Across schools, about two-thirds of students thought that they were on track to graduate on time, and about 20 percent were not sure; there was wide variation across schools.

Students reported that their school was helping them prepare for life after high school, but preparation focused more on college than career. In the survey and focus groups, a majority of students reported that their teachers made sure all students were planning for life after high school. Students said their schools offered specific college- and career-focused activities and connected them with job and internship opportunities. Students also reported that they talked with teachers about college and that they were working on skills (e.g., time management, collaboration) that they would use in college. School staff reported emphasizing postsecondary preparation activities that focused on college preparation, such as campus visits and the acquisition of content and skills that students need to be successful in college, as well as activities focused on general college and career readiness. Staff at three schools discussed activities focused specifically on career readiness.

School Operations and Management

Principals described hiring and retaining high-quality teachers and persistent teacher vacancies as challenges. In interviews, all principals said they had difficulty finding qualified teacher candidates who were a good fit for the school model, particularly in mathematics, science, and engineering. Teacher retention was mentioned as a challenge by all principals and seemed to be a particular problem in five schools, one of which, a Cohort I school, had not had a mathematics teacher since opening in 2014. Staff at three schools reported having a vacancy in at least one major teaching role for all or most of the 2015–

2016 school year. Teachers and principals said that such vacancies strained staff capacity and limited teachers' opportunities to innovate and seek support because they had to give up their planning time.

Teachers reported high levels of autonomy and input into the design and operation of their school, which can support innovation, but noted that constant innovation could be problematic. Teachers in most schools said they had significant autonomy for designing curriculum and instructional materials, choosing instructional approaches, and designing courses, adding that the ability to innovate was a valued aspect of their role. Teachers at most schools reported that they were able to provide input or raise concerns about the school model, and at two schools staff reported regular opportunities for teachers to share feedback and ideas with school leaders and implement those ideas. However, some teachers described frequent innovation as problematic, saying that it could be difficult to abandon plans or systems that they had worked hard to develop, and that innovation without adequate resources could be challenging.

Principals reported receiving helpful support and valued Springpoint support in particular. Overall, principals' perceptions of their PD experiences were generally positive, with coaching and mentoring support reported to be the most helpful. However, two less-positive areas stood out: Three of ten surveyed principals agreed that their PD helped them collaborate with students and families, and four agreed that it helped them manage school resources efficiently. Principals particularly valued Springpoint support: Nine out of ten principals reported that Springpoint's support was helpful and that they considered Springpoint to be an important partner in their work. Specifically, in interviews, most principals described the school visits and study tours with other ObD schools and the technical assistance and consulting provided by Springpoint as extremely valuable for helping them develop and refine their school models, particularly their mastery systems.

Schools were working to create partnerships to facilitate community-based learning opportunities for students and to build networks with other schools. Staff at all schools reported that developing and maintaining connections and partnerships with community-based organizations, civic leaders, and the businesses and residents around the school—and using these relationships to create learning opportunities—was an important goal. However, fewer than half of teachers reported that community members were involved in students' education, and interviews with district leaders suggested that creating these opportunities and partnerships was still a work in progress. In many

schools, staff described partnerships that were based on preexisting relationships or in reaction to student interest (e.g., finding an internship for a student interested in a certain field) but not school-wide or systematically implemented.

Although staff at all schools described interacting with other ObD schools, such interactions generally occurred when schools had mutual interests, such as similar challenges to implementing asynchronous learning. Three schools shared their building with a non-ObD school. Staff at one of these schools talked about partnering to provide extracurricular activities to students, and teachers from another school described weekly meetings with the co-located school to ensure communication and allow students from both schools to participate in electives and extracurricular activities.

Springpoint helped schools address resource limitations and improve capacity. In all sites, interviewed district leaders and school staff said Springpoint played a key role in connecting them to resources, such as other innovative schools and consultants, that they might not have accessed otherwise. School leaders mentioned that these colleagues and consultants helped them think about how best to design their mastery systems, communicate with parents, and continuously improve the school designs.

Schools revised their models based on broad feedback, but few had systematic ways to incorporate the analysis of performance data in their decisions to revise. Although most teachers agreed that the school regularly reviewed and revised the school model and used stakeholder feedback to do so, staff at only two schools mentioned systematic processes that were used to review data and make changes. In most schools, staff described responding to problems as they arose (e.g., from teacher or student feedback) rather than identifying and addressing problems through a systematic process. In addition, staff at three schools mentioned challenges associated with their efforts to continuously improve the school model. According to teachers, constant change was difficult for some students to handle and could cause burnout and fatigue among teachers.

Cross-Cohort Comparisons

Most teachers reported emphasizing mastery-based and personalized instructional practices, but Cohort II teachers reported more-extensive adoption and perceived fewer obstacles than Cohort I teachers. Ninety percent of surveyed teachers and principals agreed that their school design included a mastery-based learning model and majorities of surveyed teachers reported emphasizing mastery-based and personalized instructional practices (e.g., giving students the chance to work through material at their own pace, demonstrating mastery before moving on to a different topic, adapting course content to meet student needs and interests, and providing students with choices in topics or content). Although reported use of these mastery-based and personalized instructional practices was extensive across schools, surveyed Cohort II teachers reported greater emphasis on some practices, such as varying topics and pace and adapting course content to meet student needs. Cohort II teachers were less likely than Cohort I teachers to perceive obstacles to mastery-based and personalized instruction.

Cohort II teachers reported more teaching experience and perceived themselves to be better prepared for teaching in an ObD school than Cohort I teachers. Surveyed Cohort II teachers reported more years of teaching experience than Cohort I teachers and were more likely to report that their teacher preparation program prepared them to a large extent to teach in an ObD school. One factor that could explain this pattern is that there was high teacher turnover in many of the Cohort I schools after the first year of operation, and this may have led schools to hire less-experienced teachers. It is also possible that experienced teachers may not have applied for open positions. Also, according to our principal interviews, teacher hiring rules in two Cohort I districts restricted which teachers they could hire, potentially resulting in a staff with fewer teachers who were willing, or prepared, to teach in an innovative environment.

District Context

District context played a key role in the implementation of the ObD schools, serving as both a support and a source of challenges. In several cases, district support of the ObD schools was designed to help spread innovative practices and lessons learned across the district.

District policies related to curriculum and teacher hiring served as both facilitators and challenges to the ObD schools. While the schools benefited from the ability to select or develop curriculum materials, school staff reported that the lack of time or capacity to find or create curriculum materials was a challenge to implementing personalized and mastery-based learning. Similarly, although many districts afforded the ObD schools some flexibility in hiring staff, school and district staff members were concerned about teachers' capacity to implement personalized and mastery-based learning.

Intermediary organizations and Springpoint served as enablers by building district capacity and providing support to the ObD schools. Key supports included creating connections between the ObD schools and other innovative schools, and Springpoint-led study tours, which were structured visits to other ObD schools. Additionally, district and school leaders said Springpoint played a key role in ensuring continued focus on the ObD design principles in the face of school and district leadership turnover.

Early Lessons for the Field

Implementation Strengths

Many aspects of implementation improved over time. Cohort I teachers' opinions about PD and clarity of school mission improved from Year One to Year Two. In Year Two, schools in both cohorts were implementing numerous practices consistent with the design principles, including a clearly defined mission, mastery-based and personalized learning approaches, and a positive school climate and culture. It is possible that these improvements were due to Springpoint supports, or that schools improved their ability to use data to identify problems and continuously improve the school model or otherwise benefited from lessons learned during the first year of implementation. Also, Cohort II schools seemed to face fewer challenges than

Designing Innovative High Schools
Implementation of the Opportunity by Design Initiative After Two Years

Cohort I schools did in their first year. Cohort II staff felt more prepared to implement the ObD principles, held more-positive opinions of their schools' data systems, and reported greater adoption of personalized and mastery-based learning practices. School and district leaders found Springpoint's support—such as connections to consultants, study tours, and aids designed to align the district vision, systems, and policies to facilitate innovation—helpful.

Key Challenges

In general, Cohort II schools seemed to experience fewer challenges than Cohort I schools did in their first year. In addition to the challenges related to developing high-quality curriculum and hiring qualified staff, ensuring high-quality instruction and maintaining universally high expectations for students emerged as key challenges. A lack of curriculum materials, inadequate staffing, a need to personalize across multiple student ability levels, and a lack of clarity on how mastery should be implemented made it difficult to implement high-quality instruction. External pressure to advance students at a certain pace, wide variation in the complexity of tasks used to assess mastery, and inconsistent application of mastery-based grading systems were barriers to maintaining universally high expectations for students.

Recommendations for Supporting Continued Implementation of ObD Models

Provide teachers with support and assistance to develop and select curriculum materials. While many teachers reported positive feelings about developing their own curriculum, they also reported spending a lot of time creating or finding materials. To promote teacher autonomy and support teachers' ability to create their own materials, school and district leaders could provide additional supports for developing curriculum, such as support from external experts or more time dedicated to co-planning or vetting materials.

Ensure that teachers have access to high-quality data to implement mastery-based and personalized approaches and the support to use them effectively. Teachers need high-quality data to implement mastery-based and personalized learning but do not always have access to them. School and district leaders can play a role in ensuring that teachers have frequent access to high-quality data that are aligned with the curriculum and easily accessible.

Develop systems and processes to ensure that all students receive high-quality instruction and are held to high expectations. Across classrooms, there was great variation in the complexity of measures used to assess mastery, and how mastery was defined and measured. This variation, along with the need to personalize instruction, made it difficult for school staff to ensure that all students received high-quality instruction and were held to the same high expectations. District and school leaders could work together to put systems in place that focus on strategic staffing (e.g., team teaching, more-experienced teachers co-teaching with less-experienced teachers) and could work to develop quality curriculum, assessments, and measures of mastery. Such systems would help promote the quality of instruction and help ensure that students are held to consistently high expectations.

Offer specialized support for recruiting, hiring, and retention, while encouraging autonomy and flexibility in district policies. Many school leaders struggled to find high-quality teachers willing to work in schools implementing innovative practices, such as mastery-based and personalized learning. High teacher turnover and vacancies in high-needs subjects, such as mathematics and science, exacerbated the challenge of hiring quality teachers. District leaders could consider providing additional supports and encouraging flexibility in teacher hiring policies that could help schools recruit, hire, and retain teachers.

Consider ways to offer principals continued support beyond the first two years of implementation as they refine their models and hire new staff. The implementation of a complex innovation is an ongoing process. Cohort I schools, even in their second year of operation, were continuing to refine their school models and could benefit from continued implementation support beyond their second year. This support could take a variety of forms based on schools' needs and contexts and could include additional support from Springpoint in the form of study tours or connections to consultants, as well as targeted support from the districts. Additionally, Cohort II schools seemed to experience fewer challenges in their first year of implementation than did Cohort I schools, and some Cohort II principals said they benefited from continued interaction and support from schools with more ObD implementation experience. Therefore, one potentially valuable support for principals could be networking opportunities that allow them to learn from one another's experiences and share their own successes.

Acknowledgments

The authors are grateful to the Opportunity by Design students, teachers, and administrators who voluntarily participated in project data collection; district, Carnegie Corporation of New York, and Springpoint staff who facilitated connections with the schools and participated in interviews; and Northwest Evaluation Association staff who facilitated assessment administration and provided assessment data and analytic support. We are also grateful to the following RAND Corporation staff who contributed to the research: Andy Bogart, Amanda Edelman, Suzette Gambone, Mark Harris, Courtney Ann Kase, Stephanie Lonsinger, Melanie Rote, Anna Saavedra, Brittany Seymour, Quinton Stroud, Lindsey Thompson, Tiffany Tsai, and Elaine Lin Wang. This document benefited substantively from feedback from Gabriella Gonzalez, Betheny Gross of the Center on Reinventing Public Education, Cathy Stasz, as well as Saskia Levy Thompson and Jennifer Timm and their colleagues at CCNY. Samantha Bennett provided expert editing. Any flaws that remain are solely the authors' responsibility.

Abbreviations

CCNY	Carnegie Corporation of New York
CCSS	Common Core State Standards
ELA	English language arts
ELL	English language learner
iNACOL	International Association for K–12 Online Learning
IRQ	instructional reflection questionnaire
LMS	learning management system
NGLC	Next Generation Learning Challenges
ObD	Opportunity by Design
PBL	project-based learning
PD	professional development
PLP	Personalized Learning Platform
PYD	positive youth development

CHAPTER ONE
Introduction

High schools across the United States are working to prepare all students for postsecondary education and career opportunities that require high levels of academic, social, and emotional skills and knowledge. States, districts, and charter management organizations have enacted a variety of reforms, including the adoption of small learning communities, the development of new approaches to career and technical education, and an expansion in the availability of advanced coursework to promote increased equity in opportunity to learn. Research suggests that these reforms have been associated with improved student achievement and postsecondary attainment in many locations where they have been implemented (Kemple and Willner, 2008; Long, Conger, and Iatarola, 2012; Bloom and Unterman, 2013).

Despite these efforts to improve the quality of students' high school experiences, however, overall levels of student achievement across the United States have remained largely stagnant over the past few decades, and sizable gaps among socioeconomic and racial/ethnic groups persist (National Assessment of Educational Progress, undated). Graduation rates have improved in recent years but are also characterized by large gaps between different student groups (National Center for Education Statistics, 2016), and high levels of required remediation among postsecondary students suggest that a high school diploma is no guarantee of college readiness (Scott-Clayton and Rodriguez, 2015). Beyond the academic realm, employers have expressed concerns about inadequate development of inter- and intrapersonal skills, such as teamwork and responsibility, that are essential for effective job performance (*Are They Really Ready to Work? Employers' Perspectives on the Basic Knowledge and Applied Skills of New Entrants to the 21st Century U.S. Workforce*, 2006).

To be successful at helping prepare all students for postsecondary success, high school leaders and educators might benefit from exploring evidence-based strategies including a more rigorous curriculum, small learning communities, and an explicit focus on preparation for college and careers (U.S. Department of Education, 2016). Teachers will also need to develop the resources and skills to offer personalized learning opportunities to students so that those who are performing far below the standards have ample opportunity to catch up, while those who have mastered them are able to pursue more-advanced material (Quint, 2006; Lewis et al., 2014; Pane et al., 2015; Sturgis, 2015).

Moreover, teachers must attend not only to students' academic proficiency, but also to

ObD Design Principles

A high-performing high school . . .

1. has a clear mission and coherent culture

2. prioritizes mastery of rigorous standards aligned to college and career readiness

3. personalizes student learning to meet student needs

4. maintains an effective human capital strategy aligned with school model and priorities

5. develops and deploys collective strengths

6. remains porous and connected

7. integrates positive youth development to optimize student engagement and effort

8. empowers and supports students through key transitions into and beyond high school

9. manages school operations efficiently and effectively

10. continuously improves its operations and model (CCNY, 2013).

socioemotional competencies, such as collaboration, leadership, and resilience, to ensure students' postsecondary, career, and civic success (Pellegrino and Hilton, 2013; Soland, Hamilton, and Stecher, 2013). In fact, efforts to promote academic achievement without simultaneously addressing other aspects of youth development, such as self-regulation and growth mindsets, could be counterproductive, as research suggests these factors interact to promote successful young adult outcomes (Nagaoka et al., 2015). Successful schools are likely to be those that take a coherent approach to communicating and enacting policies and practices that emphasize high-quality, rigorous instruction and that incorporate positive youth development for all students (Lake, Hill, and Maas, 2015).

The Carnegie Corporation of New York's (CCNY's) Opportunity by Design (ObD) initiative is intended to address these ambitious goals, based on the premise that promising high school reforms need to be integrated into a comprehensive school design and accompanied by appropriate, sustained levels of financial, policy, and implementation supports (CCNY, 2013). CCNY launched the ObD initiative in 2013 to support the design and early implementation of a network of small high schools of choice that incorporate a set of ten design principles. Districts that submitted proposals were expected to situate the new schools in the context of the district's overall school improvement plan and describe how the proposed high schools would align to the design principles and help improve students' academic and postsecondary outcomes.

The proposals also needed to explain how the district would support the schools' development at a policy level (e.g., create or change policies that support mastery-based learning) and with resources to design the school models (e.g., space to work, hiring a school principal) as well as request support for specific design activities (e.g., vetting or developing curriculum materials and assessments, consulting or coaching support for the design team). Applicant districts were asked to convene school design teams consisting of the school leader, several teachers, community partners, and key district staff (e.g., curriculum writers, technology support providers) and charge these teams with developing school structures and systems that incorporated the design principles in a way that would meet the needs of the student population and district context. The design principles, if fully implemented, should result in a school that functions differently from most high schools nationally. CCNY described the rationale for the ObD schools in this way:

Nowhere is the need for redesign greater or more urgent than in American high schools. . . . [Developing new schools that make accelerated and recuperative learning pathways available to all students] will require a radical rethinking of business-as-usual school models and a decisive move away from the one-size-fits-all high schools that persist today (CCNY, 2013, pp. 1–2).

Although the ObD schools are expected to address all ten principles, CCNY has identified three "power principles" foundational to the schools' models:

- *Prioritizing mastery:* Students demonstrate deep understanding of clearly defined, rigorous competencies (see, e.g., reDesign, 2017).
- *Personalizing learning:* Student learning experiences are tailored to individual learning needs and interests.
- *Positive youth development (PYD):* Students have voice in their learning and access to experiences and relationships that help them develop the skills and mindsets to succeed (see, e.g., American College Testing for Youth, 2017, and Springpoint Schools, 2017).

The ObD initiative was designed to support start-up and early operation of these new school models. CCNY provided schools with three years of funding—for one design year prior to opening the school and the first two years of operation—with the expectation that the funding would be used to pay for start-up costs and that the schools would design their models to be self-sustaining using public funds after two years. Implementation of the ObD schools was phased—five schools opened in fall 2014, five opened in fall 2015, two schools opened in fall 2016, and the last schools will open in fall 2017. The ObD initiative also engages districts in the design process with support from a capacity-building organization, Springpoint: Partners in School Design, funded by CCNY. As part of ObD, CCNY and Springpoint provide structured, comprehensive support to school districts, charter management organizations, and intermediary organizations that seek to use innovative school design as a lever for moving student achievement and as a means of enabling broader reforms across the central office.

Support from Springpoint was designed to provide guidance regarding how to implement the design principles, along with examples of successful implementation, and the support was intended to

CCNY (2017) describes the ObD initiative as having three objectives: "1) to develop innovative school models in high-poverty areas that meet students where they are, promote student-centered learning, and serve as proof points for the field; 2) build capacity of school districts and partners to create and support schools that embody the principles in a way that is authentic to the local context; and 3) build knowledge for the field about what it takes to design, launch, and support innovative school models across a variety of contexts."

decrease as schools gained experience implementing the models. Springpoint support would be most intensive during the design year and the first year of operation, and would be provided as needed in the second year of operation. The schools in each cohort received a similar set of in-person, virtual, and individualized supports during their design years, but the supports each cohort of schools received evolved over time. For example, according to interviews with Springpoint staff, the Cohort II schools had more time for the design process than did the Cohort I schools, and the tools that Springpoint created to guide schools in their design were more developed after the first cohort. According to Springpoint staff, they provided more-tailored supports and met with design teams in smaller groups for the Cohort II schools and were more deliberate in calibrating support to each school's specific needs.

A key component of Springpoint's support included *study tours*—visits to innovative schools that were successfully implementing models aligned with key design principles. Study tours included classroom observations; conversations with teachers, students, and school leaders; and sharing of materials (e.g., mastery rubrics, student handbooks, lesson plans) so that staff from the visiting schools could understand the host school's design and, if they wished, incorporate attractive features into their own school models. After the first year of the initiative, study tours included other ObD schools to facilitate connections among the ObD schools so they could learn from each other.

CCNY intends that the ObD initiative will serve as a model for opening and supporting new schools that will enable districts and charter management organizations nationwide to develop and operate innovative school models that foster rich and effective student-centered learning environments at scale, as well as identify the contextual factors that support this type of innovation. In addition, CCNY hopes that the initiative will encourage the ObD districts to use the design principles to create additional innovative schools and ultimately spread the approach throughout the district.

Evaluation Approach

RAND began conducting a five-year formative and summative evaluation of the ObD initiative in June 2014. The evaluation is collecting data on the implementation of the school models, district context, and challenges and facilitators as well as student academic and behavioral outcomes. We collected data from the ten ObD schools open during the 2015–2016 school year. To learn about implementation, we interviewed CCNY, Springpoint, and district staff; collected artifacts; surveyed teachers and students; and collected instructional reflection questionnaires, or IRQs (brief surveys administered to teachers daily for several weeks during the school year, focusing on instruction in that day's lesson). We also visited each of the schools to interview school leaders and teachers, conduct focus groups with students and parents, and observe classrooms. The number of interview participants, focus groups, and survey response rates are summarized in Table 1.1. Additional information about all of these data-collection methods is in the appendix.

Although the ObD initiative is unique in its focus on design principles to inform the creation of new high schools that meet the needs of all students, it is one of several initiatives focused on the implementation of highly personalized and mastery-based instructional approaches. At the time ObD was being developed and rolled out, the program was one of a few other early grant programs designed to encourage development and adoption of personalized approaches—such as

Table 1.1. Number of Interview Participants, Focus Groups, and Survey Response Rates

Data-Collection Method	Source	N	Total Response Rate (%) (if applicable)	Range of Response Rates Across Schools (%) (if applicable)
Interviews	CCNY and Springpoint staff	4	—	—
	District and intermediary leaders	8	—	—
	School leaders	13[a]	—	—
	Teachers	46	—	—
Focus groups[b]	Students	10	—	—
	Parents	4	—	—
Observations	Classroom	42	—	—
Artifacts	Assignments, assessment reports	30	—	—
Surveys	Principals	10	100	100
	Teachers	61	81	60–100
	Students[c]	1,161 (fall) 1,070 (spring)	93 (fall) 88 (spring)	82–100 (fall) 70–100 (spring)
IRQs	Teachers[d]	29 (fall) 59 (spring)	83 (fall) 79 (spring)	63–100 (fall) 38–100 (spring)

[a] The school leader interview N is 13 because we requested permission to interview up to two leaders in each school. We interviewed all ten principals, and in three schools we also interviewed a second school leader (a mastery specialist, a design fellow, and a campus coordinator).

[b] Focus group N represents the number of groups, not the number of participants. Across schools, 65 students and 14 parents participated in focus groups. Only four schools provided permission to conduct parent focus groups.

[c] Response rates among students with consent.

[d] Response rates for completion of at least one of the ten IRQs.

the Next Generation Learning Challenges (NGLC) initiative,[1] and, more recently, the XQ Institute's Super Schools initiative.[2] At the time ObD was developed, there was a great deal of interest in implementing highly personalized, mastery-based approaches, but the best way to do this was not yet (and still is not) well understood, and there were limited high-quality resources available to support such innovative designs. For example, although numerous online curriculum programs were available for use in core academic subjects, few of these programs were specifically designed to support a mastery-based environment, and there was no clear way to judge the quality or effectiveness of those resources or to pull them together into a cohesive school design.

The ObD schools share some features with the NGLC schools in particular. Although the NGLC schools did not implement the ObD design principles as such, they did implement personalized and mastery-based approaches and relied on technology and frequent use of data to inform those approaches. A RAND report (Pane et al., 2015) recently examined implementation of personalized and mastery-based learning in NGLC schools, and in national comparison groups of students and teachers, using methods similar to those in this study; some of the findings from that report provide helpful context for interpreting the ObD findings. Therefore, where relevant, we provide comparable findings from the earlier RAND report, though it is important to keep in mind that the NGLC and ObD schools differ in some important ways, including the fact that the NGLC initiative included schools at all

[1] The NGLC initiative, founded in 2010, is managed by EDUCAUSE and supports school districts, charter management organizations, and partner organizations that embrace personalized learning. To be considered for funding, schools applied for a competitive grant. In their applications, schools were required to describe with specificity how their models would support personalized learning.

[2] The XQ Institute's Super Schools initiative, founded in 2016, awarded $10 million to ten high schools over five years in a competitive application process. To be considered for funding, applicants had to be high schools, serve populations of predominantly low-income and minority students, and articulate a vision of high school that focused on students' learning needs, desires, and preferences.

grade levels, not just high schools. In addition, most of the NGLC schools were charter schools, while the ObD schools are managed by school districts and, in some cases, intermediary organizations. Despite these differences, examining the areas of commonality between the two groups is one way of providing a benchmark for understanding how personalized learning approaches are implemented more broadly.

The ObD Schools

The ten ObD schools in this study, which opened in fall 2014 and fall 2015, were located in six urban districts and served large proportions of minority students from low-income families. Overall, the schools served about 1,300 students. The grade ranges and enrollments of these schools will expand in future years as they scale up to full capacity. Key sample characteristics include the following, based on 2015–2016 school year data provided by school administrators:

- The schoolwide proportion of students eligible for free or reduced-price lunch ranged from 63 to 100 percent (median: 95 percent).
- The schoolwide proportion of students of color ranged from 53 to 100 percent (median: 93 percent).
- Schools in their first year of operation had about 100 students in ninth grade only; schools in their second year of operation had an average of 175 students in grades 9 and 10.

- Half (five) of the schools had been in operation for one year and half (five) for two years:
  - **Cohort I:** the five schools in their second year of operation in 2015–2016
  - **Cohort II:** the five schools in their first year of operation in 2015–2016.

Although the schools participating in the ObD initiative were not expected to implement specific programs (e.g., specific online curricula), they were required to incorporate the ten design principles, described in more detail in later sections, into their models, and they all participated in a design year with support from Springpoint. As we described earlier, CCNY placed particular emphasis on implementation of the mastery, personalization, and PYD design principles. Each school had the flexibility to implement a model that would work best with its context, students, and goals and was expected to refine its school model over time.

Focus of This Report

This report presents findings from the first two years of ObD implementation (i.e., school years 2014–2015 and 2015–2016); future reports will explore student achievement outcomes associated with these models. We discuss the activities school staff undertook to implement the design principles, the conditions that hindered or facilitated implementation, and how school staff addressed these conditions. Although this report includes findings that pertain to all ten design principles, we emphasize the three "power principles"—prioritizing mastery, personalizing learning, and PYD—which, as we noted earlier, CCNY suggests are foundational to the schools' models. We intend that this interim report will provide formative feedback to the funder, Springpoint, and the ObD schools, and be of interest to educators and policymakers who are implementing, or considering implementing, similar reforms.

We grouped the ten design principles into two domains to provide an organizational structure for the report. The first domain, discussed in Chapter Two, focuses on the design principles that most clearly define the schools' culture and instructional approaches. Chapter Two includes five principles: clear mission and coherent culture, prioritizing mastery of rigorous standards, personalizing learning to meet student needs, PYD, and empowering and supporting students through key transitions. The second domain, discussed in Chapter Three, focuses on the design principles that articulate how the school operates and is managed. Chapter Three includes the five principles of human capital, collective strengths, remaining porous and connected, effective and efficient management of school operations, and continuous improvement. For each design principle, we provide a vignette, drawn from the interview and focus group data, which exemplifies the principle.

Although this report focuses largely on data collected during the 2015–2016 school year, we also examined how selected practices differ by cohort and experience with the model and created three groups, as follows:

1. Cohort I, 2014–2015 (serving ninth-graders)
2. Cohort I, 2015–2016 (serving ninth- and tenth-graders)
3. Cohort II, 2015–2016 (serving ninth-graders).

We present these findings in Chapter Four. In Chapter Five, we discuss district contextual factors related to implementation, and in Chapter Six we present implementation successes, key challenges, and recommendations.

The findings presented in this report comprise a synthesis of the implementation data. We rely heavily on teacher and student survey data because those sources are the most representative of teachers' and students' attitudes and perceptions. We also rely on the interviews with principals, teachers, and district staff, which, although less representative than the surveys, provide in-depth information about key aspects of implementation that can help clarify patterns in the survey data and illuminate comparisons among schools and districts. We triangulated these sources with IRQs, classroom observation, and artifact data as applicable. When we discuss the interview data, we use terms such as *many* and *most* to refer to more than half of interview respondents in the applicable group (e.g., school leaders, teachers, or district staff) across schools and districts, and we use *several* or *some* to refer to less than half of respondents. We note instances where interview findings are applicable only in specific schools or districts. Percentages reported here are based on survey results.

It is important to recognize that these findings provide an early look at the ObD models. Designing and launching new high schools is a highly complex endeavor, and we should not expect all of the design principles to be implemented in a comprehensive way at this early stage in the schools' development. It is also likely that the successes and challenges we identified during these early years will change as school leaders and staff gain experience with the models and as state and district policies are revised. Readers should also keep in mind that the data on implementation are limited by their self-reported nature and relatively small sample sizes, which are themselves limited by the size of the schools. The comparisons across years and cohorts in particular should be considered exploratory due to the small numbers of schools and teachers in each group; we did not conduct tests of statistical significance of these differences. Readers are encouraged to review the more detailed discussion of the methods and limitations in the appendix.

We also recognize that the practices described in the design principles exist on a continuum and that schools across the United States have begun adopting many of these practices even when they do not explicitly espouse personalized and mastery-based approaches. The ObD schools were among the early adopters of these innovative practices, and while we would expect to see these practices implemented to a greater extent in the ObD schools than in traditional schools, there is not necessarily a clear distinction between what constitutes "typical" practice and what constitutes practices aligned with the design principles. Without a national comparison group, we are not able to determine whether the practices, facilitators, and challenges reported by ObD staff and students were substantively different from those used and experienced by educators and students nationally.

Moreover, as personalized and mastery-based learning approaches become more popular, it may become more difficult to discern differences between the ObD schools and schools nationally. As such, the discussion of implementation in this interim report is largely descriptive. Despite these limitations, these formative data allow us to provide detailed examples of the design principles in the ObD schools and rich descriptions of implementation facilitators and challenges and to examine areas of similarities and differences across schools and districts with a view to providing early lessons for the field.

CHAPTER TWO
Culture and Instruction

Design Principles Addressed in This Chapter

- Clear mission and coherent culture
- Prioritizing mastery of rigorous standards
- Personalizing learning to meet student needs
- Positive youth development
- Empowering and supporting students through key transitions

KEY TAKEAWAYS

- School missions were clear and aligned with the design principles, but few schools had mechanisms for ensuring that key aspects of the model were regularly monitored to guarantee effective implementation.

- Teachers reported emphasizing, and students reported experiencing, mastery-based and personalized instructional practices.

- Key challenges to mastery and personalization included inconsistent expectations for mastery, varying access to data, external pressure to advance students at a certain pace, and the significant time required to create instructional materials.

- Online curricula facilitated some aspects of mastery-based and personalized learning, but were inadequate as a stand-alone instructional tool.

- All schools made efforts to promote PYD and to integrate it into academic structures.

- Staff and students reported positive school climates but noted that climate was also an area for improvement.

- Most students reported that they received help with planning their high school experience, but about one-quarter were not sure whether they were on track to graduate on time.

- Students reported a strong emphasis on college preparation and less focus on career preparation.

Summary

The ObD schools seemed to have good conceptual foundations for implementing the design principles—school staff described missions aligned with the design principles and emphasized mastery-based instruction, socioemotional and academic learning, and working with underserved populations. Most schools seemed to struggle with ensuring that key aspects of the model were regularly monitored to ensure effective implementation, perhaps because most schools did not have clear monitoring mechanisms in place.

Across schools, most teachers and students reported mastery-based and personalized learning practices in their classrooms. Practices such as thoughtful use of online curricula and assigning more than one instructor to a classroom appeared to facilitate personalized approaches. Teachers and principals noted tensions between faithful implementation of mastery-based approaches and making adequate curriculum progress and expressed a need for improving the consistency and rigor of tasks assessed for mastery. Teachers reported varying access to the data required to effectively implement mastery-based and personalized practices and that the significant time required to create suitable instructional materials was a key challenge.

The ObD school designs emphasized PYD and integrated it into academic structures as part of the mastery and personalization systems, which were designed to facilitate student choice, take students' interests into account when designing lessons or projects, provide tailored supports, and emphasize high expectations. But school staff described PYD in terms of structures and systems for supporting a positive school climate, encouraging students to improve their behavior, and providing a way for students to give feedback, rather than as a component of academic structures. Students and staff reported positive school climates, but staff also noted that it was an area where they could still improve, particularly in terms of student discipline and the right level of engagement with external partners and community members.

Students reported that school staff members were helping them plan their high school experiences with a view to preparation for postsecondary success. Most students reported that they believed they were on track to graduate on time but about one-quarter were unsure, and there was wide variation across schools. School staff reported emphasizing postsecondary preparation activities that focused on college preparation, such as college visits and the acquisition of content and skills needed to be successful in college; there was less focus on explicit career preparation.

Clear Mission and Coherent Culture

Design Principle 1: A high-performing secondary school has a clear mission and coherent culture that is evidenced by a clearly defined purpose, goals, and school culture. The school's mission and culture are embodied in all aspects of school design.[1]

---

[1] The definitions of the design principles provided in this report were developed by CCNY.

Key Findings on Clear Mission and Coherent Culture

Most schools had clear missions that were consistent and aligned with the design principles. In the site visit interviews, school leaders described missions focused on empowering students by soliciting their ideas and incorporating these into the

VIGNETTE: What does a clear mission and coherent culture look like?

School F, a Cohort II school, clearly described its vision, mission, and school values in its vision statement: "To empower all students to own their learning, shape their dreams, and create a better world." The vision statement was visible in all of the classrooms and hallways; most teachers recited the vision during interviews and shared how the mission and vision were pervasive in all aspects of the school.

The school's mission and culture were embodied in all aspects of the school through what the staff described as four drivers—advisory, grade-level team meetings; student agency; data-driven instruction; and competency-based education—which they monitored to ensure they were aligned with the mission and consistent with the school culture. School staff said each of the drivers was integral to the school model, clarifying that as long as the drivers were being successfully implemented, the school would achieve its mission and vision. The school had developed rubrics and benchmarks to measure progress on each of the drivers and inform changes when the benchmarks were not being met.

"We started with a vision that was really wordy, then we created our competencies, then after refining and refining, we got down to the essence. The mission part of it, how do we do it, is about everything that we do, [including] all of our systems. . . . All of those things are aligned to our vision and are what create our culture."
—SCHOOL F TEACHER

school design, providing for them academically and emotionally, and preparing them for life after high school. Across schools, most principals' and teachers' descriptions of their school's mission and vision emphasized mastery, socioemotional and academic learning, and working with underserved populations. Across schools, nearly three-quarters of surveyed teachers agreed that their school had a clear mission. When asked to describe their school's mission and vision, school staff generally provided descriptions consistent with both other staff's descriptions and the school's mission statement. In addition, at least one teacher at every school talked about his or her school's mission or specific elements of the school model as a reason they applied to work at the school.

Few schools had mechanisms for ensuring alignment between the mission and the school design. In interviews, staff at three schools described processes by which staff monitored alignment between school mission and design. Staff at these schools talked about using rubrics to rate the extent to which the mission was embodied in school design and the provision of professional development (PD) to help staff implement the mission. Staff in schools with dedicated district-level support staff (e.g., mastery specialists or some similar support) talked about how

"Every few months we sort of realize we might be drifting away from [the mission statement], and we do a pretty good job of monitoring that as a school. . . . A lot of our work this year has been around making sure that the decisions that we're making are coming from our mission statement, and it's not just coming down from the administration."

—COHORT I SCHOOL LEADER

helpful they were in improving alignment between mission and design.

Aligning the school design with the mission was a challenge in most schools. Despite widespread agreement that their school's mission was clear and grounded in the design principles, staff members in only one of the ten schools were able to describe how the school model was aligned with the mission; that is, how key aspects of the school model supported the mission and were regularly monitored to ensure

effective implementation. For example, in interviews, the teachers, principal, and district staff affiliated with this school spoke in detail about how they tried to make every aspect of the school design align to, and support, the school mission. In contrast, teachers at the other nine schools talked about struggling to align their school model with the mission. Although school staff did not explicitly make this connection, it is possible that the absence of clear mechanisms for ensuring alignment between mission and school design contributed to this challenge in many schools.

Prioritizing Mastery of Rigorous Standards

Design Principle 2: A high-performing secondary school prioritizes mastery of rigorous standards aligned to college and career readiness and has a curriculum that enables all students to meet rigorous standards, multiple opportunities for students to show mastery through performance-based assessments, and student advancement based on demonstration of mastery of knowledge and skills.

Key Findings on Prioritizing Mastery of Rigorous Standards

Mastery-Based Instructional Practices

Most teachers and students reported engaging in mastery-based instructional practices. Fifty-six to 89 percent of surveyed teachers reported using a number of practices consistent with mastery-based instruction, such as giving students the chance to

---

VIGNETTE: What does prioritizing mastery of rigorous standards look like?

School C is a Cohort I school in which students worked toward mastering specific *content standards* as well as *skill standards* that were content-neutral and involved Common Core State Standards (CCSS)-aligned reading and writing skills as well as general academic behaviors (e.g., note-taking, organization).

Students demonstrated their mastery of these standards by completing tasks called "at-bats," which included simple online quizzes and more-complex performance-based tasks. Students had three opportunities, or at-bats, to demonstrate mastery of each standard. The school's vision was that at-bats should be rigorous and aligned to college-level capabilities, available to students at any time, and designed to meet students' individual learning needs.

Teachers assessed the extent to which students had mastered each skill using a rubric ranging from one to five. Mastery was defined as an average score of three on the three most recent at-bats. In mathematics and history classes, students used online curricula and advanced through the content at their own pace. In these classes, students could attempt at-bats when they were ready and advance to new class content when they demonstrated mastery. By the middle of the spring semester, several students had already earned course credit and advanced to the next course. Students at School C were expected to monitor their work and present their progress to their families and their teachers. The intention was to help make the mastery-based system of advancement transparent to students and families and enable students to take responsibility for their own learning.

"I took the [state test] early in Global History, so [my teacher] assigned me to an Edgenuity course 'cause he doesn't want me taking the class since I tested out of the class. I proved proficient in that class."

—SCHOOL C STUDENT

---

work through material at a faster or slower pace than other students, reviewing material until they fully understood it, requiring that students demonstrate mastery before they could move on to a different topic, and allowing students to work on different topics or skills at the same time. Further, 90 percent of teachers and principals agreed that their school design included a mastery-based learning model. Fifty-nine percent of surveyed students reported that they had opportunities to practice material until they fully understood it most of the time or always. Similarly, 56 percent of students reported that they were required to show they understood a topic before moving on to the next topic. Most students who participated in focus groups agreed.

Teachers reported that students needed to adjust to mastery-based learning. Students who are not accustomed to a mastery-based instructional environment might need time and guidance to become comfortable with demonstrating their learning in multiple attempts over time. Teachers in several schools said they struggled to help students understand the rationale for demonstrating mastery with this approach. For example, many teachers reported that students often became upset when they perceived that they were given more, or different, work than others. Many teachers perceived that students were more interested in the instant gratification of getting a good grade and did not understand that they might have to revise their work when they did not attain mastery right away. In schools where one aspect of mastery was flexible deadlines designed to provide students with multiple opportunities to revise, most teachers said this signaled to students that they could turn their assignments in whenever they wished. According to these teachers, an unintended consequence of this approach was that many students often waited to turn in assignments until right before grades were due. These teachers added that this was not the intention, and that it left these students with no time to revise their work.

Assessment and Data Use

Mastery was assessed using a variety of methods, which in some cases could contribute to inconsistent or low expectations. To engage in mastery-based instruction, teachers need methods and tools for assessing students' competency and using the resulting data to determine whether students should move on to new material. Research suggests that high-quality assessments that provide real-time data, along

> *"There is not a consistent meaning of mastery. I think there is just a big learning design curve [when it comes to defining mastery]. . . . We're letting students move on to other levels before they achieve mastery [for ninth grade]—Level 9. If [students] really want to get a nine, they know what they need to do. But, we're not always going through that cycle to make sure [students] get there. I think it's just us [staff] trying to figure out how to work it all out."*
>
> —COHORT I TEACHER

with reporting systems that facilitate use of those data, are particularly crucial for informing instructional practice (Coburn and Turner, 2012; Hamilton et al., 2009). Both across and within schools, tasks used to assess mastery varied in terms of scope and quality. Across schools, teachers and school leaders expressed a need for improving the consistency and rigor of tasks assessed for mastery. In two districts, tasks assessed for mastery were generally described by teachers as summative performance tasks or projects that took place after students had spent some time learning content or practicing skills. In the other four districts, teachers described using a range of assessment types to determine mastery, ranging from quick online quizzes and worksheets to larger projects.

In addition, some teachers mentioned a need for more clarity in both the definition of mastery and also in the alignment of rubrics used to assess mastery and noted that the criteria for mastery used in their school did not always set a high bar for student work. For example, one school defined mastery as "students must master 65 percent of the standards at a Level 3 or better," and in another school growth scores were used as one component of determining mastery. In three schools, teachers and leaders alluded to inconsistent expectations for tasks that assess mastery, saying that some staff assigned mastery tasks that were low in rigor (e.g., worksheets, short quizzes) or inconsistently applied the mastery standard (i.e., expected higher-level work from some students but not from others). Even in the three schools where teachers did not explicitly mention it, this inconsistency was evident in teachers' reports of using tasks of varying quality and rigor.

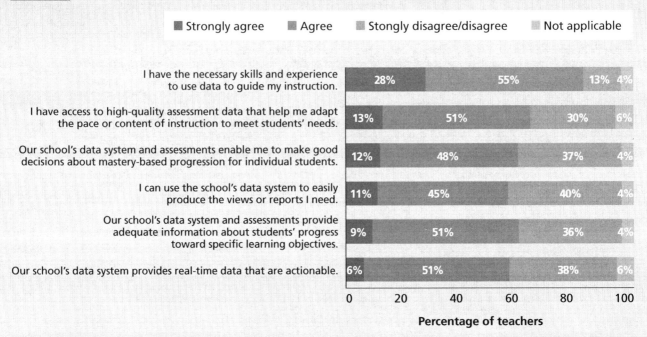

FIGURE 2.1

Teachers' Agreement with Questions About School Data Systems, Spring 2016

Legend: ■ Strongly agree ■ Agree ■ Stongly disagree/disagree ■ Not applicable

Statement	Strongly agree	Agree	Stongly disagree/disagree	Not applicable
I have the necessary skills and experience to use data to guide my instruction.	28%	55%	13%	4%
I have access to high-quality assessment data that help me adapt the pace or content of instruction to meet students' needs.	13%	51%	30%	6%
Our school's data system and assessments enable me to make good decisions about mastery-based progression for individual students.	12%	48%	37%	4%
I can use the school's data system to easily produce the views or reports I need.	11%	45%	40%	4%
Our school's data system and assessments provide adequate information about students' progress toward specific learning objectives.	9%	51%	36%	4%
Our school's data system provides real-time data that are actionable.	6%	51%	38%	6%

Percentage of teachers

NOTE: Survey question: Please indicate your agreement with each of the [above] statements. Responses were given on a 5-point scale where "Not applicable" = 0 and "Strongly agree" = 5. N = 53. Some rows do not sum to exactly 100% due to rounding.

Most teachers reported using school data systems to inform instruction, but frequency of access to data varied. For example, 64 percent of teachers agreed that they had access to high-quality assessment data they could use to adapt the pace or content of instruction to meet student needs, and 56 percent agreed that they could use their school's data system to easily produce the reports they needed, as shown in Figure 2.1.

Most surveyed teachers reported receiving various types of achievement data (e.g., student performance on specific concepts or skills, identification of specific students who need extra assistance) at least monthly, but many teachers expressed a need for more or better data. Half of teachers and four out of ten principals reported that lack of high-quality measures of mastery was an obstacle to mastery-based instruction. In interviews, some teachers in schools that used long-term performance tasks indicated the need for more-frequent data when using such tasks. These teachers said they struggled with gauging how students were doing as they worked on the task. Some of these teachers developed "exit tickets" (i.e., short, frequent quizzes) or other workarounds to provide them with a sense of students' formative progress, but in general

reported that they had to wait for data from the summative task to assess student progress.

When compared with teachers in the NGLC study, ObD teachers reported receiving data less frequently but using it to inform their instruction to a greater extent. This suggests that ObD teachers understand the value of using data to inform mastery-based practices but might benefit from data systems or employing practices or assignments that provide data more frequently.

Standards and Curriculum

Many teachers described tension between mastery-based approaches and making adequate curriculum progress. None of the ObD schools used a system for student advancement that was wholly mastery-based, and teacher and principal discretion was a factor in student advancement decisions in all schools. Across schools, many teachers said they felt pressure to move through the curriculum at a pace sufficient to expose all students to the course content, thus limiting students' ability to master the material by working at their own pace. Some teachers also reported that they felt pressure to prepare students for accountability assessments, and this could be one reason teachers felt the need to progress through the curriculum at a consistent pace. In addition, many teachers reported struggling to provide students with multiple attempts to demonstrate mastery, especially in schools that did not make extensive use of online curricula or in which there was only one teacher per classroom. Teachers' comments and survey responses suggest that pressure to cover all the course material within the year, poor student attendance, and limited work completion were among the challenges to offering multiple attempts for mastery.

Most schools were experimenting with their mastery and grading policies with the goal of balancing the need for students to demonstrate learning with completing high school in four years. According to all principals, large percentages of their students were not learning at grade level; principals said they were trying to balance the need to help students catch up with teaching grade-level content and ensuring graduation in four years. However, most principals reported feeling pressure to ensure that students graduated within four years, which they noted was contrary to mastery-based principles. In a mastery-based system in which students progress only when they have demonstrated that they understand the material, it could take some students more than four years to complete high school, particularly if students enter high school behind grade-level. To several principals, it was clear that if they adhered strictly to mastery-based principles and allowed students to work at their own pace and not advance until the content had been mastered, then large percentages of students would not graduate in four years. These principals felt that taking more than four years to complete high school would not be acceptable to parents or the district and were struggling with how to address this challenge.

In the early years of implementation, extensive use of teacher-created materials and projects could limit the extent to which students could progress at their own pace. Most of the ObD schools partly relied on teacher-created instructional materials. In the early years of ObD implementation, this could limit student advancement, because students can advance only as far as the existing materials and content can accommodate. Similarly, many teachers noted that heterogeneously grouping students for projects, which many teachers considered an important part of project-based learning (PBL), could limit the

"Because if you are truly following the competencies as they are laid out, and you do not progress until your competencies are met, that means high school can look something like five or six years. That is not the mindset of the community—you go to high school for grades 9 through 12, four years."

—**COHORT I PRINCIPAL**

extent to which students were able to work at their own pace. According to teachers, projects often required some amount of instruction to the class as a whole to introduce the topic and content of the project. When working on projects, teachers described the need to move students along so that they could be exposed to the relevant content and participate in the project even if they had not mastered previous material.

Use of online curricula has the potential to facilitate some aspects of mastery-based instruction, but some teachers expressed concerns about quality. Advancing to new material upon demonstrating mastery of certain skills and standards is an important aspect of a mastery model. According to teachers and students, online curricula allowed students to advance at their own pace, largely because the curriculum was fully developed and students didn't have to wait for the teacher to develop the next lesson or assessment. In one school that used online curricula for history and mathematics classes, students in these classes could advance and earn course credit as they mastered standards. However, two other schools that relied heavily on online curricula for delivering course content in the first year of operation decided to scale back their use in the second year, due to negative feedback from students and low student completion of course material. Although many teachers we interviewed were concerned that the online curricula used in their schools were of low quality, utilizing online curricula (at least to some extent) seems to be the only approach thus far that allowed students to truly progress (or focus on needed standards) at their own pace.

Personalizing Learning to Meet Student Needs

Design Principle 3: A high-performing secondary school personalizes learning to meet student needs such that instruction is offered in a variety of learning modalities; linked to students' strengths and learning goals; data-driven, with real-time feedback for students and teachers; and incorporates embedded, performance-based formative assessments. Technology is used effectively to facilitate anytime, anywhere learning.

Key Findings on Personalizing Learning to Meet Student Needs

Teachers reported practices consistent with personalized learning. Majorities of teachers reported that they emphasized practices consistent with personalized learning to a large or moderate extent, as shown in Figure 2.2.

Teachers reported that the need to create personalized instructional materials was a key challenge to personalizing learning for students. In interviews, teachers and principals in all but one school described the lack of time to develop

---

VIGNETTE: What does personalizing learning to meet student needs look like?

School F is a Cohort II school that served ninth-grade students. Teachers used a variety of techniques to personalize learning opportunities for students. An online tool called the Personalized Learning Platform (PLP), which delivered content in the form of *playlists*, assessed students and provided real-time feedback to students and teachers. Students controlled the pace of their learning and moved through playlists independently. When students completed a playlist, they took diagnostic and content assessments to see if they were ready to move on to a performance-based task. The assessments helped students monitor their own learning by providing real-time feedback about their mastery of the material.

Teachers also received real-time data about student learning and used these data to make instructional decisions. In addition to viewing student scores on diagnostic and content assessments, the PLP included checklists for larger performance-based tasks that allowed teachers to track student progress as they completed each step of the task. Teachers also completed data driven inquiry cycles to look for trends in student performance and group students based on their progress toward larger tasks. Additional time for personalized learning was built into the schedule in the school's "Flex Block" period. During Flex Block, students were grouped for remediation or enrichment in groups that changed every two weeks.

Students had some choice in their learning opportunities and could opt to join accelerated *AP cohorts* in many of their classes. The cohort option was designed to help teachers meet the needs of a wide range of learners in one classroom. Cohorts were flexible, and students had opportunities to join the AP cohort throughout the year. AP cohorts were taught in a more asynchronous, student-directed style, while the non-AP cohorts were more teacher-led.

"On the PLP, when you click on the playlist, there is a diagnostic assessment that you can take that tells you what you need to work on exactly. . . . If you get 2 out of 2 then it means you are good on that subject and that you can move on [to take the content assessments], but if you have a 0 out of 2, then that means you need to work on it more."

—SCHOOL F STUDENT

FIGURE 2.2

Extent to Which Teachers Reported Emphasizing Practices Consistent with Personalized Learning, Spring 2016

■ Emphasized to a large extent   ■ Emphasized to a moderate extent
■ Emphasized to a small extent   ■ Have not emphasized

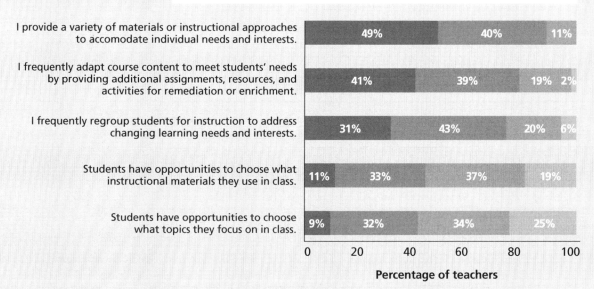

	Large	Moderate	Small	Not
I provide a variety of materials or instructional approaches to accomodate individual needs and interests.	49%	40%	11%	
I frequently adapt course content to meet students' needs by providing additional assignments, resources, and activities for remediation or enrichment.	41%	39%	19%	2%
I frequently regroup students for instruction to address changing learning needs and interests.	31%	43%	20%	6%
Students have opportunities to choose what instructional materials they use in class.	11%	33%	37%	19%
Students have opportunities to choose what topics they focus on in class.	9%	32%	34%	25%

Percentage of teachers

NOTE: Survey question: "We recognize that adopting personalized and mastery-based learning approaches requires teachers to change their instruction in many ways, and that teachers might emphasize some aspects of personalization and mastery more than others. In this question, we are interested in learning the extent to which you have emphasized the [above] elements of personalization and mastery so far. Please indicate the extent to which you emphasize the following approaches." Responses were given on a 4-point scale where "Have not emphasized" = 0 to "Emphasized to a large extent" = 3. N = 53–54. Not all rows sum to exactly 100% due to rounding.

personalized materials as a challenge, and 65 percent of surveyed teachers reported that it was a major or minor obstacle. One possible reason for this finding, according to teachers, is that their districts provided relatively few curriculum materials. This finding is consistent with results from national surveys that indicate that teachers typically search for materials from a wide variety of sources, including online lesson plan banks as well as general-interest sources such as Pinterest (Kaufman, Thompson, and Opfer, 2016). The recent transition to new standards in many states, combined with the challenges associated with finding materials to support high levels of personalization in the ObD schools, have placed heavy demands on many teachers to put together a curriculum that meets students' needs. Time to develop personalized lessons emerged as an obstacle in other studies of personalized learning (Pane et al., 2015).

Principals corroborated teachers' reports that finding or creating high-quality curriculum materials was a key challenge. Several principals reported concerns about teachers' capacity to create and implement high-quality personalized curriculum materials, largely because teachers were inexperienced,

"Doing online work isn't as beneficial to our success as in-class work, because being online makes it easier for a student to find shortcuts. You can go online and look up answers. So when you take the state test for graduation, all those tests that you looked up the answers for and didn't learn the information don't help you, unlike in a real class when you have to write notes and turn it in to the teacher."

—**COHORT I STUDENT**

because teaching in a personalized environment was new to most teachers, and because creating a curriculum is very time-consuming. Although some teachers said that having to build their own curriculum limited the extent to which students could learn asynchronously, others said they appreciated the freedom and flexibility to create their own curriculum.

Online curricula can support personalization, but are not adequate as stand-alone instructional tools without supplemental teacher support. Overall, surveyed teachers reported that their technology-based materials were of high quality and reported using online curricula, programs, and resources as one way to facilitate personalized learning. For example, many teachers noted that online programs offered students access to personalized content and data on student progress and allowed

students to progress at their own pace. But some teachers admitted relying too heavily on online programs and expressed concerns about quality of student learning experiences. In two schools, online curricula were used to address staff shortages. In these schools, students learned science and mathematics using an online curriculum and were supervised by substitute teachers and, when available, school staff. Students recognized the limitations of learning exclusively by computer, and two Cohort I schools scaled back their use of online curricula in their second year of operation (2015–2016), largely in response to student feedback.

Some schools relied on extra classroom staff to support personalized learning. Teachers and principals in three schools reported that having two teachers in a classroom helped instructors address the learning needs of students at different levels of mastery. In one school, teacher residents from a local university were present in many classrooms. Teachers at this school said working with the residents helped them differentiate for all students at once. During our class observations, both the teacher and resident delivered instruction simultaneously to separate groups of students. Similarly, two schools used co-teachers (two certified teachers) in English classrooms. These co-teachers said the presence of the other instructor helped them both provide targeted support to students and facilitate instruction for students at different levels of mastery. Leaders at these schools agreed. Of course, this type of staffing can require extra resources and might not be feasible in all schools implementing personalized learning.

Positive Youth Development

Design Principle 7: A high-performing secondary school integrates PYD to optimize student engagement and effort in a way that fosters caring, consistent student-adult relationships that communicate high expectations for student learning and behavior; allows adults to communicate clear expectations for student competencies and standards of performance; and provides opportunities for students to contribute to the school environment and have a voice in decisions. The school also encourages student responsibility for meeting learning and personal goals, openness to and encouragement of family participation, and integration of community participation, assets, and culture.

Key Findings on Positive Youth Development

All schools made efforts to promote PYD and had some mechanism for students to provide input. School leaders and teachers at all ten ObD schools affirmed that they were making efforts to promote PYD, and many staff said it was part of the school's mission and vision. Staff talked about creating a positive school climate, creating student leadership teams, and using PYD as a means of encouraging students to improve their behavior. But, according to teacher interviews, in the majority of schools, these efforts did not always seem to be systematic

VIGNETTE: What does positive youth development look like?

According to the principal and teachers at School E, a Cohort I school, students had an important voice in the school and in their own learning. Students could provide input to teachers in their *advisory* (i.e., the groups in which students met each morning to focus on building socioemotional skills, building relationships with teachers, and reviewing their progress in school), and representatives from each advisory shared students' opinions and ideas with school staff. It was also common for students to contribute to the school environment by starting clubs.

The school encouraged student responsibility for meeting learning and personal goals and communicated its high expectations when it reorganized classes so that they were grouped by level of student independence rather than by learning level. In spring 2016, the school began grouping students in three levels—teacher-directed, teacher-supported, and semi-autonomous—based on the extent to which the student was comfortable learning independently. The school planned to create a fourth group (autonomous) when students were ready. Ideally, students would learn the value of being independent and progress to the more autonomous groupings over time. Students were assigned to the same group for all of their core courses and received personalized support based on which group they were in. Students were also assigned *accountability partners*—a group in which students would help each other set goals and track their progress toward those goals.

The school made an effort to foster caring, consistent student-adult relationships through advisory sessions, in which students talked about any issues they were having and built relationships with staff. School staff described engaging parents by sharing information about student progress. Families could access the online grading system to view student assignments and grades, and the school held quarterly progress conferences with parents. The school was in the process of creating a parent organization.

"I have the most independent kids, but I feel like it is beneficial for them in terms of positive peer pressure of how quickly and well the kids in your classes are working. I've been glad to use the [classroom] downstairs because there's a lot of space and freedom. For my teacher-supported class, the class [room] is a little smaller, so I provide more support."

—SCHOOL E TEACHER

or consistent across the school. All schools had some way—and some schools had multiple ways—for students to provide input, but these mechanisms varied in formality. Formal means included student surveys and some type of student council or student leadership team. Informal mechanisms included "open-door" policies, where students were broadly encouraged to talk to staff about questions or issues. Staff at one school reported that their receptiveness to student input led to adjusting their allocation of instructional time to balance direct instruction with independent practice using online software.

All schools incorporated aspects of PYD in mastery and personalization structures, but in general, school staff described PYD as distinct from academics. All the school designs incorporated PYD in their mastery and personalization systems by facilitating student choice, taking students' interests into account when designing lessons or projects, providing tailored supports, and emphasizing high expectations, as intended by the design principle. But in interviews, school staff did not describe PYD as integrated with mastery and personalization. Instead, staff described PYD as separate from academics. Staff at eight schools described advisory as the main method of promoting PYD. Advisory was characterized as a nonacademic period that focused on building the school community and relationships with students, tracking student progress, giving students an opportunity to provide input, and providing time for students to focus on developing socioemotional skills. In addition, staff at all schools mentioned extracurricular activities that were either available to all students or designed based on students' interests as a mechanism for promoting PYD.

"We had students, about a third of the way through the year, tell us that there's too much computer time and they miss direct-instruction time. We actually said okay and had a big meeting where we invited parents, students, and teachers where we talked about it and we saw a change pretty immediately after that."

—**COHORT II TEACHER**

All schools said they made efforts to engage parents and community members and promote transparency; parents agreed. Teachers and principals at all the schools said they aimed to make student progress transparent and used a variety of methods to communicate progress with students and families. For example, three schools had a staff member whose full-time job was parent and community engagement; this person also worked to identify external opportunities (e.g., internships) for students. Staff and parents at these schools reported that this role was important and the person in the role was effective.

A key way most schools engaged parents was by providing updates on student progress, generally by encouraging parents to access the online grading system, as well as through emails, conferences, mailings home, and phone calls. In addition, parents who participated in the focus groups said they felt that the opportunities to get involved with the school were there even if they did not always take advantage of them. Most parents agreed that teachers and administrators were responsive and available when they needed them.

Staff and students reported positive school climates. All principals, and almost all teachers, agreed that students respected each other, respected school staff, and were motivated to achieve. Large majorities of teachers and principals agreed that teachers were focused on student learning and believed all students could be college-ready. Similarly, a large majority of students agreed that their opinions were respected; teachers paid attention to all students, not just top students; all students were encouraged to go to college; and that at least one adult knew the student well, as shown in Figure 2.3.

Maintaining consistently high expectations for all students was challenging. Although a majority of students agreed that the adults in their school had high expectations for them, some principals and teachers expressed concern that expectations for students were not consistently applied. For example, in three schools several staff members were concerned that some adults had lowered their expectations for some students because these students came from disadvantaged backgrounds. Even when most staff reported that the adults in the school had high expectations for all students, some teachers said expectations weren't applied consistently in terms of scoring student work. For example, a score of two on the rubric could mean

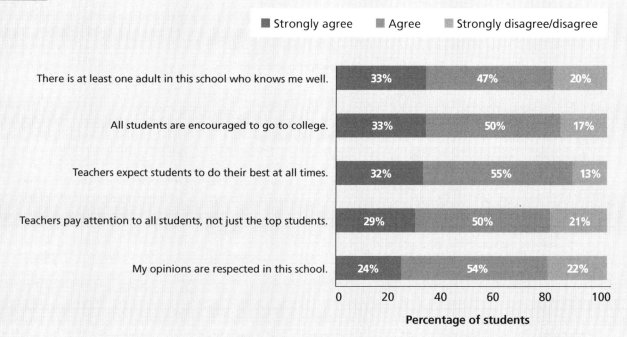

FIGURE 2.3 **Students' Perceptions of School Climate, Spring 2016**

■ Strongly agree   ■ Agree   ▦ Strongly disagree/disagree

	Strongly agree	Agree	Strongly disagree/disagree
There is at least one adult in this school who knows me well.	33%	47%	20%
All students are encouraged to go to college.	33%	50%	17%
Teachers expect students to do their best at all times.	32%	55%	13%
Teachers pay attention to all students, not just the top students.	29%	50%	21%
My opinions are respected in this school.	24%	54%	22%

Percentage of students

NOTE: Survey question: "How much do you agree with the [above] statements about your school?" Responses were given on a 4-point scale ranging from "Strongly disagree" = 1 to "Strongly agree" = 4. N = 975 to 977.

different things for different teachers and for different students.

School staff described PYD as an area where they had made strides but could still improve, particularly in the area of school climate. Most teachers and school leaders in both cohorts agreed that the climate and culture in their school had improved. For example, one teacher said that expectations for student behavior had become more consistent and were being more consistently applied by teachers. A school leader noted that school climate improved and disciplinary incidents declined when the school began grouping students by level of autonomy rather than learning level. However, most teachers and school leaders agreed that although many aspects of PYD had improved, there was still room for growth, particularly in the areas of parent engagement and outreach—specifically providing services to parents—improving school climate, communicating high expectations to all students, and communicating student progress to students and families.

Staff at most schools characterized creating a positive climate as an area of improvement and mentioned mechanisms for doing so (e.g., restorative

"We've recently been trying to make [PYD] an explicit goal. I am facilitating the student leadership team. . . . It's really been a chance for students to become leaders and think of an idea, follow it through and be able to . . . collaborate on things and think about all of the stuff we want students to be able to do that [is] not academic. PYD has been presented to students as the intangibles we don't explicitly teach, things like leadership, community responsibility, and collaboration."

—COHORT II TEACHER

justice, student leadership teams). At seven schools, staff said that creating a positive climate and culture was a top priority. Several principals characterized the need for improvement as foundational: Once they got the culture and climate "right," they said, everything else would fall into place.

Empowering and Supporting Students

Design Principle 8: A high-performing secondary school empowers and supports students through key transitions (i.e., into and beyond high school) such that explicit linkages between future academic and career pathways and current learning and activities are apparent, and there is transparency regarding student status and progress toward graduation for students and parents or guardians.

Key Findings on Empowering and Supporting Students

Most students reported receiving help to plan their high school experience, but substantial percentages in some schools did not know whether they were on track to graduate. About 80 percent of students reported that they had discussed—briefly or in depth—topics such as the classes they should take throughout high school, the classes they should take this year, the level of mastery they should achieve in each subject to be on track to graduate, and experiences they should try to get outside of school. Across schools and cohorts, 62 percent of students thought they were on track to graduate on time, while 22 percent were not sure. However, there was some variation across cohorts: Among ninth-graders, Cohort II students were more likely than Cohort I students to report that they believed they were on track to graduate from high

---

VIGNETTE: What does empowering and supporting students through key transitions look like?

School F, a Cohort II school, empowered students by helping them understand their options after high school and by making student progress transparent. Through a partnership with a local community college, students could receive college credit in high school, and all students took a course—for college credit—about the skills needed to be successful in college. School leaders wanted students to graduate from high school with 12 college credits, which would make them eligible for a free year of college tuition at any state school. According to many students and parents, receiving college credit in high school was one of the biggest benefits of, and reasons for, attending that school.

The school emphasized careers by offering students a choice of three pathways, or majors, (STEM, engineering, social entrepreneurship) designed to help them in future careers. The school selected courses, such as computer programming and engineering, which would introduce students to potential careers, and during the year all students participated in job shadowing and visited at least two colleges.

Students and families had access to student progress in the PLP, the school's learning management system (LMS). The PLP showed students how they performed on specific assignments over the course of the year. The PLP's red wrench icon helped students and parents identify areas students needed to work on to progress on their learning targets. Students tracked their progress in the PLP and checked in with teachers about their progress every morning during advisory.

"[T]he idea is that if you've done career exploration, you know who you are. . . . In 10th grade, students will pick an elective that is either a teacher preparation class or business entrepreneurship class or a graphic design class. . . . So then in 11th [grade], they will be able to say whether they want to lean toward a more humanities or more STEM path. We will work to secure them an internship related to the career sector they are interested in pursuing. . . . Most high schools, you aren't that way. You are a generalist all the way through, and you're a generalist for the first half of college."

—SCHOOL F PRINCIPAL

---

school on time (72 percent compared with 53 percent). Students' responses to this question also varied widely by school, as shown in Figure 2.4.

Students reported that their school helped them prepare for life after high school. Eighty-three percent of students agreed that teachers make sure all students are planning for life after graduation. At eight schools, students who participated in focus groups said that their schools were preparing them for life after high school to some extent. Students cited specific college- and career-focused activities, such as job and internship opportunities, discussions with teachers about college, and the ability to work on skills that they will use in college, to support this opinion. School staff reported emphasizing postsecondary preparation activities that focused on college preparation, such as college visits and the acquisition of content and skills that students need to be successful in college. One school identified itself as an Early College school, and two schools talked about providing students with opportunities for earning college credit during high school. Staff at many schools described activities focused on general college and career readiness, and staff at three schools discussed activities focused specifically on career readiness.

> *"Sometimes I talk to certain teachers about what I want to be, and they'll help me out and get people to come down and talk to me. Some teachers get medical people to come down to talk to kids interested in being doctors."*
>
> **—COHORT I STUDENT**

Partnerships focused on career experiences were guided by student interests, but opportunities did not seem to be systematic. Teachers and leaders at six schools said they worked with partners to introduce students to different careers or provide students with internship, job, and volunteer opportunities. Five of the ten schools had staff in dedicated positions, such as partnership coordinator, guidance counselor, and dean of engagement, whose goal was to help identify outside partners and connect students with internships and job opportunities. Although a number of students said that school staff connected them to career opportunities they

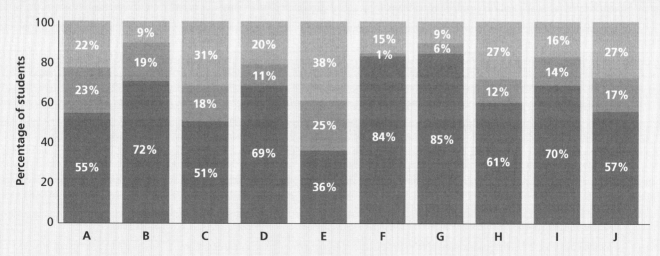

FIGURE 2.4 **Students' Beliefs About Whether They Were on Track to Graduate from High School on Time, by School, Spring 2016**

Legend:
- I am not sure whether I am on track to graduate on time
- I do not think I am on track to graduate on time
- I think I am on track to graduate on time

School	I think I am on track	I do not think I am on track	I am not sure
A	55%	23%	22%
B	72%	19%	9%
C	51%	18%	31%
D	69%	11%	20%
E	36%	25%	38%
F	84%	1%	15%
G	85%	6%	9%
H	61%	12%	27%
I	70%	14%	16%
J	57%	17%	27%

NOTE: Survey question: "Based on the classes you have taken and your performance in those classes, which of the [above] statements best describes your current situation?" Responses were given on a 3-point scale ranging from "I am not sure whether I am on track to graduate high school on time" = 1 to "I think I am on track to graduate high school on time" = 3. N = 56 to 150. Schools A–E are Cohort I schools; schools F–J are Cohort II schools. Not all columns sum to exactly 100% due to rounding.

were interested in, it appeared that most schools lacked a systematic way of connecting all students to opportunities of interest. Instead, the opportunities mentioned by staff and students appeared to be created ad hoc, either when student interest arose or when an external connection presented itself. In one school, for example, students who participated in the focus group mentioned that a local construction company had come to the school to interview students for summer jobs because the owner of the company was connected to a teacher at the school.

CHAPTER THREE
School Management and Operations

Design Principles Addressed in This Chapter

■ Effective human capital strategy

■ Collective strengths

■ Remaining porous and connected

■ Managing school operations efficiently and effectively

■ Continuous improvement

KEY TAKEAWAYS

■ Principals described hiring and retaining high-quality teachers and persistent teacher vacancies as challenges.

■ Teachers reported high levels of autonomy and input into the design and operation of their schools, which can support innovation, but noted that constant innovation presented challenges.

■ Principals reported receiving helpful supports and valued Springpoint support in particular, but they felt least prepared to implement and support mastery systems.

■ Schools were working to create partnerships to facilitate community-based learning opportunities for students and to build networks with other schools.

■ Springpoint helped schools address resource limitations and improved capacity.

■ Schools revised their models based on broad feedback, but few had systematic ways to incorporate the analysis of performance data in their decisions to revise.

Summary

All ObD principals described challenges in hiring and retaining high-quality teachers as a barrier to effective implementation. Persistent teacher vacancies were described as a problem in five schools, and in three of these schools teachers reported that vacancies strained staff capacity and limited their ability to collaborate and innovate. Teachers reported receiving a variety of supports and that most of them were helpful, particularly informal collaboration with colleagues and common planning time, but access to these supports varied. Many teachers reported high levels of autonomy to develop curriculum, choose instructional materials, and design courses and noted that this was a valued aspect of their role. Teachers at most schools reported high levels of input into the school model and operations but noted that constant change and innovation could be difficult without adequate resources to develop or implement new ideas. Principals' perceptions of their PD experiences were generally positive. They found particular value in Springpoint's school visits and study tours with other ObD schools. Principals reported that they felt least prepared to support teachers to implement mastery learning and to design a mastery-based school model.

Creating partnerships that would support community-based learning opportunities was a goal at all the schools, but these partnerships were still a work in progress. ObD school leaders did not report much collaboration with other ObD schools outside of the Springpoint study tours, but the ObD schools that were co-located with a district school described strong partnerships with those schools. District and school staff in all sites said that Springpoint played a key role in connecting them to resources, such as other innovative schools and consultants that they might not have had access to otherwise. All the ObD schools used stakeholder feedback to make changes to the model, but few schools had systematic processes for making changes. One possible reason so few schools had developed systematic processes for continuous improvement is that coming up with such a system may not have taken priority in these early years of implementation, when schools were trying to develop systems for everyday operation. In most schools, staff described responding to problems as they arose rather than identifying and addressing problems through a systematic process.

Effective Human Capital Strategy

Design Principle 4: A high-performing secondary school maintains an effective human capital strategy aligned with the school's model and priorities. The human capital strategy includes consistent, high-quality systems for sourcing and selecting teachers and staff; individualized PD that cultivates teachers' strengths and meets school needs and priorities, including use of blended learning; fair and equitable teacher evaluation; leadership development opportunities; and a leadership pipeline.

Key Findings on Effective Human Capital Strategy

Principals described hiring and retaining high-quality teachers as a challenge. All the ObD principals reported difficulty finding qualified

VIGNETTE: What does an effective human capital strategy look like?

School B is a Cohort I school that serves ninth- and tenth-grade students. According to district and school leaders, teacher recruitment and retention has been a district-wide challenge, and the school has struggled to fill vacant teaching positions and retain staff. District leaders reported that they were working with Springpoint to design a strategic plan to address these issues district-wide and in School B.

When hiring teaching staff, the principal of School B looked for candidates with a passion for developing students, a skill that he believes cannot be taught. The school's student council was included in the hiring process and had the opportunity to rate candidates' performance in teaching sample lessons.

The ObD schools in this district provided regular PD opportunities for teachers. Students went to school for two months at a time, followed by a three-week break. During the third week of each break, teachers met for a week of PD. School B teachers felt that the weeklong sessions, along with leadership support, helped them implement what they learned in PD.

Teachers in School B received PD aligned to specific school goals and to the design principles, such as sessions that focused on unit planning, creating rubrics aligned to competencies, and PBL. These sessions were supplemented with follow-up support and coaching from the district's mastery specialist and a consultant, who helped to facilitate the sessions and worked with teachers to develop both the competencies and a common language to facilitate their use. A PBL consultant provided in-depth training, coaching, and opportunities for teachers to receive support in planning projects and implementing them in class.

"I [told teacher candidates that I] needed more than just you teaching content. I need you to build my students and show them how to be successful. You have to show them how to do it. I feel that the people I picked up have a heart for this. I can teach you how to teach but I can't teach the heart."

—SCHOOL B PRINCIPAL

candidates who were a good fit for the school model, particularly in mathematics, science, and engineering. Principals sought teacher candidates with some (e.g., three to five years) teaching experience, strong instructional skills, and personal traits or work habits that aligned with the school design, but they varied in the extent to which they emphasized those things; some principals valued experience more than instructional skills, for example.

Teacher retention was mentioned as a challenge by all principals and seemed to be a particular problem in five schools, one of which, a Cohort I school, had not had a mathematics teacher since opening in 2014. In three schools, leadership turnover seemed to be related to low teacher retention. Staff in schools that experienced principal turnover described difficulties resulting from these leadership transitions as contributing to teacher dissatisfaction. In one school, we learned that most of the teaching staff planned to leave because the principal was leaving.

Teachers' access to helpful supports varied. Most surveyed teachers reported that informal collaboration with colleagues and common planning time were the supports received most frequently and perceived

"I knew that [the principal] wouldn't stay forever, but the [principal leaving after two years] caught me off guard. Some [teachers] had already made their moves and some, like me, made them after we found out [the principal] was leaving, since I know we don't get to pick our new principal. Yes, it's 95 percent of it. I don't want to do this without [principal] unless you find someone who gets it and can follow through."

—COHORT II TEACHER

as most helpful. Most teachers reported receiving a variety of supports and finding most of them helpful, as shown in Figure 3.1. District PD stands out as an exception; nearly one-quarter of teachers reported receiving it and finding it unhelpful. Although only 55 percent of teachers reported receiving feedback from other teachers, the vast majority of the teachers who received this support indicated that it was helpful;

FIGURE 3.1 Teachers' Reports of Receipt and Helpfulness of PD, Spring 2016

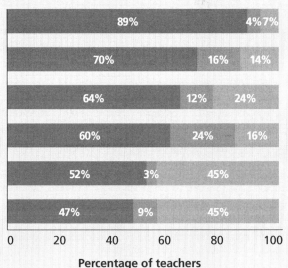

■ Received and somewhat or very helpful
■ Received and unhelpful
■ Not received

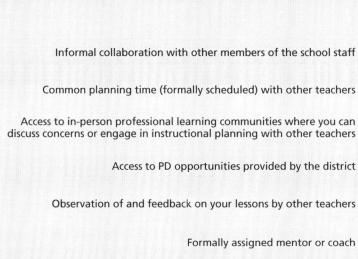

	Received and somewhat or very helpful	Received and unhelpful	Not received
Informal collaboration with other members of the school staff	89%	4%	7%
Common planning time (formally scheduled) with other teachers	70%	16%	14%
Access to in-person professional learning communities where you can discuss concerns or engage in instructional planning with other teachers	64%	12%	24%
Access to PD opportunities provided by the district	60%	24%	16%
Observation of and feedback on your lessons by other teachers	52%	3%	45%
Formally assigned mentor or coach	47%	9%	45%

Percentage of teachers

NOTE: Survey question: "Please indicate whether, in the past year, you received each of the [above] kinds of supports, and the extent to which you found it helpful for improving your instruction." Response options were given on a 4-point scale ranging from "Not received" = 0 to "Received and found very helpful" = 3. N = 55–58. Scores of 2 and 3 were combined into one "somewhat or very helpful" category. Not all rows sum to exactly 100% due to rounding.

"We have a week to work with specialists about what to improve upon or something new [every PD session]. I have never felt so supported. . . . When you come from a suburban school they have their way of doing things, so you go to a PD and you don't change. But here you can actually implement [what you learn in PD]. I think our PD is great."

—COHORT I TEACHER

this suggests that peer feedback is a valued approach to professional learning and should perhaps be made available to more teachers. Teachers who participated in interviews reported that the most common PD topics included those related to mastery, personalization, or use of a LMS. Although many schools built time for PD into the school schedule, usually in the form of an early-release day for students, teachers reported that this time wasn't always well used. Perhaps as a result, teachers varied in the extent to which they felt supported by the school's PD opportunities, as well as the extent to which they played a role in shaping or delivering PD.

Principals reported receiving helpful supports and valued Springpoint support in particular.
Principals found coaching and mentoring support to be the most helpful. Few principals reported receiving coaching and mentoring from other ObD principals, but those who received such support reported that it was helpful. Few principals reported receiving district PD or coaching specific to ObD schools. Overall, principals' perceptions of their PD experiences were generally positive, but two less positive areas stood out: Only three of ten principals agreed that their PD helped them collaborate with students and families, and four agreed that it helped them manage school resources efficiently. Principals felt least prepared to support teachers to implement mastery learning and to design a mastery-based school model.

In interviews, school and district leaders said they considered Springpoint to be an important partner in their work. Specifically, most principals described the school visits and study tours with other ObD schools and the technical assistance and consulting provided by Springpoint as valuable and very helpful. Most

"I think the way we collaborate is by learning through Springpoint about best practices that are happening so it saves us time, that's how we get things. The collaboration is filtered through Springpoint because they know what we need, and they know what these other schools have."

—COHORT II SCHOOL LEADER

principals also noted that in general, the district PD they received was aligned with Springpoint supports, which helped them formulate next steps, and emphasized that they valued Springpoint's feedback and growing knowledge of their district and ObD school(s).

Collective Strengths

Design Principle 5: A high-performing secondary school develops and deploys collective strengths such that teaching in teams strengthens instructional design and delivery and enables professional growth. School designs should include mechanisms that promote opportunities for innovation and initiative among teachers and staff. Differentiated roles for adults (e.g., multiple "teacher" roles) enable effective implementation of the school model.

Key Findings on Collective Strengths

Most teachers reported high levels of autonomy and input into the school design and operations, which can support innovation. Eighty-five percent of surveyed teachers agreed that their school promoted innovation and initiative, and 80 percent said they would feel comfortable raising concerns about their school with administrators. In interviews, teachers in eight schools said that they had significant autonomy for designing curriculum and instructional materials, choosing instructional approaches, and designing courses. Several of these teachers said that the ability to innovate was a valued aspect of their role. All the teachers we interviewed at six schools said that they were able to provide input or raise concerns about the school model, while teachers at the other four schools expressed mixed opinions. Staff at two of the six schools where teachers said their input was valued described formal ways teachers could share feedback with administrators. One principal described

---

VIGNETTE: What does developing and deploying collective strengths look like?

At School F, a Cohort II school, the model promoted teacher teaming and staff innovation and utilized differentiated roles for teachers (e.g., some teachers served dual roles as administrators or lead teachers). Teachers participated in weekly grade-level team meetings, which alternated between engaging in a data-driven problem-solving process and an assignment-tuning protocol every other week. During the assignment-tuning protocol, teachers discussed and provided feedback on one another's assignments in an effort to strengthen instruction.

According to teachers, constant innovation was an important part of the school model. Teachers had the autonomy to design their own courses and curriculum and took turns leading PD sessions. The principal and other school leaders regularly collected teacher input through a feedback loop created when leaders met weekly with their staff.

Distributed leadership—in which teachers hold key leadership roles—was an important component of the school model. The principal used federal grant dollars to fund leadership positions, such as assistant administrator, dean of curriculum and instruction, and dean of culture, for experienced teachers. Less-experienced teachers interested in leadership roles could participate in "stepping stone" roles, such as facilitators or new teacher ambassadors, to gain leadership experience. The principal said these leadership roles have helped attract strong teacher candidates.

"It is a distributive leadership model. First of all, we are building the strengths of our own in-house leadership, building the capacity for everyone who is a leader. There are five of us on the leadership team. There is the principal, there is another administrator who also plays a role of the DR [differentiated roles]. . . . The three of us who are DRs, it's just a really strong leadership team. We are also just enough in the classrooms that we also support teachers and students."

—SCHOOL F TEACHER

"Our coach from reDesign—who was supposed to be our curriculum coordinator and give instructional support—became a de facto assistant principal, and we're all short-handed. . . . Because we're all being stretched thin, I don't have a lot of coaching support. I'm used to people coming into my room and giving me feedback and helping me grow as a teacher . . . ."

—COHORT I TEACHER

a "feedback loop" created when school leaders met weekly with the teachers they supervised and then with each other, providing teachers with a regular opportunity to share feedback and ideas with school leaders and implement those ideas.

A few teachers described frequent innovation as problematic, saying that it was sometimes difficult to abandon plans or systems that teachers had worked hard to develop, that "innovating," or creating a curriculum "from scratch" was challenging and time-consuming without a model to follow, and that innovation can be challenging without adequate resources to develop or implement new ideas.

Persistent teacher vacancies strained staff capacity and the ability to collaborate. Staff at three schools reported having a vacancy in at least one major teaching role for all or most of the 2015–2016 school year. One principal said these vacancies strained staff capacity because other teachers were responsible for covering the class, and because it limited teachers' ability to consistently implement new systems. In another school, teachers said that the lack of substitutes limited their capacity to innovate because when a teacher was absent, other teachers had to give up their planning period to cover the absent teacher's class. As a result, it was difficult for teachers at this school to find time to observe one another's classrooms and learn from each other's practice. In addition, teachers in these three schools said gaps in the teaching staff resulted in supporting staff (e.g., counselors, coaches, social workers, English language learner [ELL] facilitators) being stretched too thin to provide the level of support that students needed.

Remaining Porous and Connected

Design Principle 6: A high-performing secondary school remains porous and connected such that it cultivates and maintains effective partnerships with organizations that enrich student learning and increase access to community resources and supports. The school should also participate in a network of schools that share knowledge and assets.

Key Findings on Remaining Porous and Connected

ObD schools are building community partnerships to create learning opportunities for students and to support staff to implement and improve the school design. A key aspect of remaining porous and connected is developing and maintaining connections and partnerships with community-based organizations, civic leaders, as well as the businesses and residents in the school community, and using these relationships to create learning opportunities. Creating such learning opportunities was a goal at all the schools, but fewer than half (47 percent) of teachers reported that community members were involved in students' education. In interviews, most district leaders expressed varying opinions about the success of partnerships at their schools, suggesting that these partnerships were still a work in progress.

Staff described two types of partnerships, those that focused on student support and those that provided professional development or improved the school design. These partnerships were initiated by the schools and were independent of their partnership with Springpoint. Partnerships focused on student support created opportunities for students to explore college or careers, designed extracurricular programs, supported student learning in the classroom, and provided supports to students and their families. But, in many cases, these partnerships were developed

---

VIGNETTE: What does remaining porous and connected look like?

School G, a Cohort II school, primarily served recent immigrants and ELL students. District staff described it as a community-based school where external partners were very important. One of the school's three core values was collaboration, which staff described as including interactions between teachers, students, and community partners. School G had multiple partnerships with external organizations that offered extracurricular activities for students; provided students with opportunities to explore colleges and potential careers; and provided health, legal, and social services for students and their families. One of the school's largest partnerships was with an immigrant services and advocacy organization that helped the school meet the needs of students and their families through activities such as workshops and wrap-around supports.

Additionally, staff at the school described working with other schools, both in the ObD network and in an intermediary organization's network, as an important aspect of the model. Since the school served primarily ELL students, many staff felt that these networks were particularly valuable for sharing lessons related to implementing the design principles for an ELL population.

"[We have] a lot of leadership opportunities outside of school as well. I was invited to speak at [an external event] and brought a student with me. There are a couple of students leading a youth-against-tobacco program in the county. There's actually a group [external organization] I'm meeting up with at lunch today who are looking to hire [student] soccer counselors for a camp this summer, and so there are all sorts of opportunities for our students to engage with the community as a whole. If we are going to be a community school, it's those things that make or break us as our kids get older. Otherwise we are just a traditional public high school doing the same thing that every other public high school does."

—SCHOOL G TEACHER

based on preexisting relationships or in reaction to student interest (e.g., finding an internship for a student interested in a certain field) and were not school-wide or systematically implemented. Partnerships focused on school improvement included providing professional development and resources, such as consultant services or coaching, to help develop and provide feedback on the school's model.

Co-location can be an opportunity for schools to collaborate and learn from each other. Staff at all schools described interacting with other ObD schools. In general, such interactions occurred when schools had mutual interests, such as similar challenges to implementing asynchronous learning. Springpoint study tours to other ObD schools were the most frequently mentioned opportunity for ObD schools to

interact with each other and staff who mentioned this said they found the study tours helpful. However, three ObD schools shared their building with a non-ObD school and staff at these three schools talked about partnering with these co-located schools. For example, one principal described partnering with her co-located school to provide extracurricular activities to students, and another described weekly meetings with the co-located school to ensure communication and allow students from both schools to participate in electives and extracurricular activities, including sports, music, and ROTC (Reserve Officer Training Corps). Another principal talked about working with district middle schools to strategically recruit students, and a teacher discussed how some of her students were involved in tutoring students at a nearby middle school.

Springpoint connected the ObD schools to resources (e.g., other schools, consultants) they might not have had access to otherwise. District leaders and school staff in all sites talked about how Springpoint played a key role in connecting them to resources, especially other innovative schools and consultants, that they might not have had access to otherwise. For example, one district leader spoke of learning about how other innovative schools implemented competency trackers, awarded credit in a mastery-based system, and communicated with parents. Several principals and staff talked about visiting innovative schools in their own and other districts, and how helpful those visits were as they developed and refined their school models. Similarly, one principal talked about attending the International Association for K–12 Online Learning (iNACOL) conference and talking with and learning from staff at other high schools attending that conference.

"Yes. I would say [working with community and external partners] is another area that we're hoping to see even more significant growth in. . . . I would say they have been very entrepreneurial about taking advantage of partnerships and overtures by community persons to be engaged with the schools. I would say that is more episodic than truly long-term strategically planned, so that's where we're trying to get them to be."

—COHORT I DISTRICT LEADER

Managing School Operations Efficiently and Effectively

Design Principle 9: A high-performing secondary school manages school operations efficiently and effectively such that time, people, and technology are used purposefully to optimize teachers' ability to support student learning; all elements of school design are organized to maximize efficient use of resources, scheduling is flexible and customized; there are clear operational performance goals and accountability mechanisms; and basic tasks are automated whenever possible.

Key Findings on Managing School Operations Efficiently and Effectively

About two-thirds of teachers across cohorts agreed that school operations were effectively and efficiently managed. Seventy percent of teachers agreed that basic tasks were automated

> *"The school schedule has been a hot mess. . . . It's very time-consuming. We had a schedule where the classes weren't the same size or didn't meet for the same number of minutes. The blue group didn't meet on Fridays so were 45 minutes less than everyone else. That made it so they didn't get to do a lot of things because we meet less with them. We've changed a great deal since the beginning. Some of it is better, and some of it is different. We haven't gotten worse. It has gotten better."*
>
> —COHORT II TEACHER

VIGNETTE: What does managing school operations efficiently and effectively look like?

Staff at School F, a Cohort II school, emphasized the importance of effectively and efficiently managing school operations and described a variety of mechanisms used to do so. After researching different LMSs, School F decided to use PLP, an LMS developed by a national charter organization and available at no cost, provided the school agreed to implement some basic tenets of the charter organization's model. The school made this choice in part because the LMSs used by other ObD schools were expensive and did not provide the functionality the staff needed, so the school decided to use a system that would be financially sustainable in the long term.

The school also used residents at local colleges and paraprofessionals to ensure that there were two adults in every classroom and students were provided personalized support. In some cases, this allowed classes to split into two sections, where one adult worked with advanced students and the other worked with the remainder of the class.

In spring 2016, the school adjusted the scheduling process to improve efficiency and more effectively personalize learning. In the new schedule, the last period of the day consisted of electives twice a week and additional support in core subjects three days a week. Every two weeks, teachers reviewed student progress and scheduled students into classes to receive either remediation or enrichment.

"So our approach to the school operations has been to be pragmatic, to borrow, and to turnkey whatever we can. But we've held to our own vision, and we've held to iNACOL's definition of competency. We basically rearranged all the parts. I don't really care about the theory; I care about the day-to-day experience of the kid."

— SCHOOL F PRINCIPAL

where possible, and 65 percent agreed that use of time, people, and technology were optimized to support student learning. Interviews suggested that the extent to which school operations were managed efficiently and effectively varied across districts. In one district, the principal and district staff said that the principal had a high degree of autonomy and the ability to choose from a menu of district services, which enabled him to manage school operations efficiently. In another district, a school leader said that the school's innovative status precluded using a number of district tools and resources, requiring them to search for other solutions, which were not as effective or efficient.

Flexible and customized scheduling was an area of growth for most schools. Five of the ten ObD schools did not have flexible scheduling (i.e., scheduling did not change frequently based on data),

and the other five schools limited flexible scheduling to one class period (e.g., a period where students could opt to work with any teacher based on their performance). Staff in four schools talked about more-traditional methods of providing flexibility in the school schedule, such as scheduling classes in a way that two teachers can work with the same group of students during a class period, thus providing more flexibility. Most school staff reported that flexible scheduling was difficult and time-consuming and were concerned that student needs could fall through the cracks. School staff also said that flexible scheduling was made difficult by district or state policies such as seat time and course progression requirements, union rules such as the length of the school day, and logistical factors such as staffing and funding.

Continuous Improvement

Design Principle 10: A high-performing secondary school continuously improves its operations and model such that performance data and analytics are used to improve curriculum and instruction, and there is regular review and revision of the school's operations and model to increase effectiveness.

Key Findings on Continuous Improvement

A majority of teachers agreed that school staff engaged in continuous improvement, but few schools had systematic processes for making changes. Seventy-seven percent of teachers agreed that the school staff regularly reviewed and revised the school model. In interviews, staff at all schools shared examples of changes and improvements they had made to their school models, but staff at only two schools mentioned that systematic processes were used to review data and make changes. Principals in both of these schools described continuous improvement as one of their schools' guiding principles and as an important component of the school's design and culture. Staff in one of these schools mentioned a strong "feedback culture" that involved frequent discussions about how to improve implementation. In the other school, the principal described an emphasis on ensuring that staff are "flexible and nimble." One possible reason so few schools had developed systematic processes for continuous improvement is that coming up with such a system may not have taken priority in these early years of implementation, when schools were trying to develop systems for everyday operation. In most schools, staff described responding to problems as they arose (e.g., from teacher or student feedback) rather than identifying and addressing problems through a systematic process.

Most schools used stakeholder feedback to make changes to the model. Staff at five schools talked specifically about soliciting and using stakeholder (e.g., student, parent, and community partner) feedback to

---

VIGNETTE: What does continuous improvement look like?

Staff at School G, a Cohort II school, described a culture of continuously reviewing practices and processes and making improvements when needed. School G staff used school- and classroom-level data to improve the school model and instruction. For example, each week, staff at School G reviewed data on students' mastery of content to identify successful and unsuccessful practices. School staff used this process to identify and address problems with the school's mastery and personalization systems. For example, during one data review session, staff recognized that students were learning at very different levels, and many were not successful with existing supports. After reviewing the data, staff identified three groups of students, those who were below mastery, those who were at mastery, and those who were beyond mastery.

Teachers then looked at the specific needs of each group of students and created the ACE (accelerate, collaborate, engage) process for personalizing learning. With this model, teachers used data to identify how students were performing on specific learning targets and provided more tailored supports based on those needs (i.e., students who have not achieved mastery *engage* with the teacher in direct instruction, students who are in the middle *collaborate* with other students to achieve mastery, and students who have achieved mastery already *accelerate* by working on more-challenging material).

"Every Thursday . . . we would bring in mastery data and start [analyzing the data]. From there, it's identifying trends, and it's also isolating what's working and what's not working. When we figure out what works, it then turns into how can we replicate it? When we figure out what doesn't work, it's figuring out how to eliminate it or fix it so it does work. . . . It's solution-oriented conversations using data."

—SCHOOL G TEACHER

"The constant push for improvement after improving so much from where we started already is a little challenging. I'm my hardest critic, but it's getting to the point where we are all declining in terms of energy level to be able to create and iterate, especially because things are working now. We just need to sit with that for a minute and see how it feels."

—COHORT II TEACHER

improve their schools' models, and staff at six schools talked about working with district, partner, and teaching staff to use data to identify areas of need for PD. In one example, staff from an intermediary organization described observing teachers in one school twice per month and using that information to help the school identify trends and areas that

could be addressed through PD. Teachers at another school mentioned a similar process of observing their colleagues' classrooms as a way to determine PD needs, and a district leader said that the PD the district provided was based partially on the needs of the ObD schools. Principals at three schools indicated that consultants helped them identify areas of improvement and planning for the next year.

School staff identified multiple challenges to continuous improvement of the school model.
Staff at three schools mentioned challenges associated with their efforts to continuously improve the school model. For example, teachers at these schools mentioned that frequently occurring changes were tough to monitor, and there was a risk that some things could fall through the cracks. Teachers at several schools described how constant change was difficult for some students to handle because school systems and processes changed just as students became accustomed to them. Finally, some teachers suggested that constant change could cause burnout and fatigue among teachers.

CHAPTER FOUR

Cross-Cohort Comparisons

In this chapter, we discuss how selected practices differ by cohort and experience with the model and create three groups:

1. Cohort I, 2014–2015 (serving ninth-graders)
2. Cohort I, 2015–2016 (serving ninth- and tenth-graders)
3. Cohort II, 2015–2016 (serving ninth-graders).

These findings are organized in the same way as those in the earlier chapters, and the ten design principles are grouped into two domains. *Culture and instruction* includes five principles: clear mission and coherent culture, prioritizing mastery of rigorous standards, personalizing learning to meet student needs, PYD, and empowering and supporting students through key transitions. *School management and operations* includes the five design principles of human capital, collective strengths, remaining porous and connected, effective and efficient management of school operations, and continuous improvement.

KEY TAKEAWAYS

- Cohort II schools reported stronger or more-intensive implementation than Cohort I schools in many areas, including mastery-based and personalized instructional approaches.
- Among Cohort I schools, implementation in many areas improved over time.

Summary

Cohort II schools reported stronger implementation of mastery-based and personalized instructional approaches and appeared to adopt such practices more readily than the Cohort I schools. However, it is possible that the differences in implementation and reported challenges across cohorts were the result of variation in contextual factors. Cohort II teachers were less likely than Cohort I teachers to report obstacles to mastery-based and personalized instruction, such as lack of curriculum flexibility, student absenteeism and discipline, pressure to cover material for standardized tests, and scheduling constraints. Cohort II teachers reported more teaching experience, perceived themselves to be better prepared for teaching in an ObD school, and were more likely to agree that aspects of their school's operations were managed effectively and efficiently than Cohort I teachers.

Over time, Cohort I schools improved in several key areas, such as clarity of school mission and implementation of two key personalized learning practices—frequent regrouping and giving students opportunities to choose the instructional materials they use in class—both of which were reportedly slightly more common in 2016 than in 2015. Cohort I teachers reported receiving more support—such as common planning time, a formal mentor or coach, and opportunities to observe other teachers—and finding them more helpful in their second year of operation (2015–2016) than in their first year.

Culture and Instruction

Clarity of school missions improved over time.
Across schools, nearly three-quarters of surveyed teachers agreed that their schools had a clear mission, although interviewed teachers at two Cohort I schools reported that their school's mission was unclear. When asked to describe their school's mission and vision, school staff generally provided descriptions consistent with both the mission statement and the descriptions by the other staff in that school. This is in contrast to what we heard during the first year of operation in Cohort I schools, in which staffs' descriptions of school missions in the interviews were more varied

and less clearly aligned with the mission statements. In addition, at least one teacher at every school talked about their school's mission or specific elements of the school model as a reason they applied to work at the school.

"For the first half [of the school year] we didn't have the competencies. . . . We had a mastery specialist come in and rework those competencies, and it's [the list of competencies] now focused on math practices that can apply to lots of situations. It's not about concepts anymore but about skills."

—COHORT I TEACHER

Cohort II schools appeared to adopt mastery-based practices more readily than Cohort I schools. Cohort II teachers were more likely than Cohort I teachers to report varying topics and pace and allowing students to work on different material at the same time to a great extent, as shown in Figure 4.1. Although reported use of these mastery-based practices is extensive across schools in both cohorts, Figure 4.1 shows that Cohort II teachers reported more-extensive use than did Cohort I teachers in 2016 and in 2015. In addition, both principals in one Cohort I district said they did not begin to "tackle" mastery until the second semester of their first year of operation (i.e., spring 2015), and that they revamped their entire mastery system in the second semester of their second year of operation (i.e., spring 2016), when the district hired a mastery specialist to help them. Two other Cohort I principals discussed the need to make sure the quality of instruction and assignments

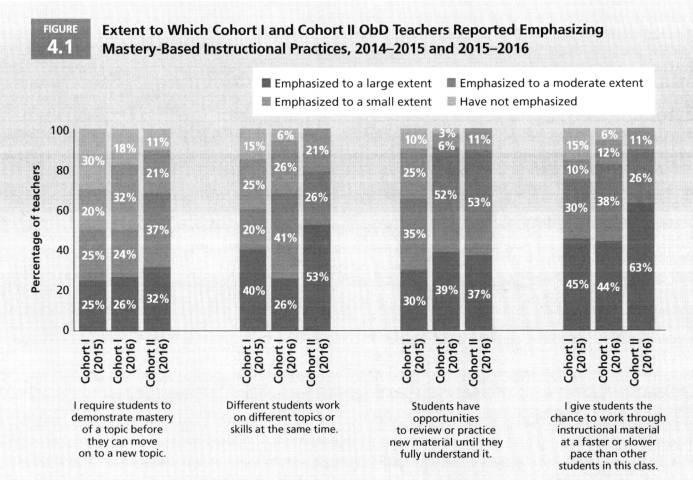

FIGURE 4.1

Extent to Which Cohort I and Cohort II ObD Teachers Reported Emphasizing Mastery-Based Instructional Practices, 2014–2015 and 2015–2016

- ■ Emphasized to a large extent
- ■ Emphasized to a moderate extent
- ■ Emphasized to a small extent
- ▨ Have not emphasized

NOTE: Survey question: "We recognize that adopting personalized and mastery-based learning approaches requires teachers to change their instruction in many ways, and that teachers might emphasize some aspects of personalization and mastery more than others. In this question, we are interested in learning the extent to which you have emphasized the following elements of personalization and mastery so far. Please indicate the extent to which you emphasize the following approaches." Responses were given on a 4-point scale from "Have not emphasized" = 1 to "Emphasized to a large extent" = 4. Cohort I (2015) N = 20, Cohort I (2016) N = 35, Cohort II (2016) N = 18. Not all columns sum to exactly 100% due to rounding.

Designing Innovative High Schools
Implementation of the Opportunity by Design Initiative After Two Years

was consistently high, and one principal said he and the staff were still experimenting with the best way to help students plan and track mastery. This suggests that Cohort II teachers used these practices to a similar or larger extent than did Cohort I teachers in their first year of school operation as well as in their second year of school operation.

Cohort II teachers reported more-frequent receipt of data that identified students who achieved mastery and that provided information on student performance on specific concepts or skills. Cohort II teachers were also more likely to agree with items related to use of data for instruction, suggesting Cohort II teachers might have slightly more-positive opinions about the quality of their data for informing instructional decisions. Cohort I schools were adopting new data systems mid-year in 2016, and teachers' unfamiliarity with the new systems could have contributed to their less favorable opinions.

Teachers' perceptions of obstacles to mastery-based instruction differed between cohorts and across years. Cohort II teachers were less likely than Cohort I teachers to report obstacles to mastery-

based instruction, such as lack of curriculum flexibility, student absenteeism and discipline, pressure to cover material for standardized tests, and scheduling constraints. Cohort II teachers perceived these conditions to be less of an obstacle than did Cohort I teachers in 2016, and Cohort I teachers perceived these obstacles to be greater in 2016 than they were in 2015. For example, in 2015, about 25 percent of Cohort I teachers reported that high levels of student absenteeism and high levels of student disciplinary problems were major obstacles to mastery-based instruction. In 2016, about 60 percent of the Cohort I teachers reported that these factors were major obstacles, compared with 22 percent of Cohort II teachers.

Many of the obstacles reported by ObD teachers were similar to those reported by NGLC teachers and teachers nationally (Pane et al., 2015). In 2016, Cohort I ObD teachers were more likely than NGLC teachers to report problems with discipline and absenteeism—NGLC teachers and teachers nationally reported these factors as obstacles in similar proportions to Cohort II teachers—but this could be because ObD schools were somewhat more likely than NGLC schools to

FIGURE
4.2
Cohort I and Cohort II Teachers' Perceptions of Obstacles to Personalizing Learning for Students, 2014–2015 and 2015–2016

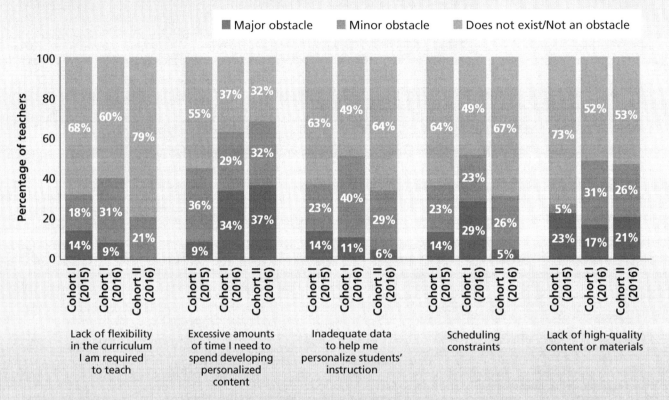

NOTE: Survey question: "Please indicate the extent to which each of the [above] conditions is an obstacle to your efforts to promote personalized learning for students." Responses were given on a 4-point scale from "Does not exist" = 0 to "Major obstacle" = 3. Cohort I (2015) N = 22, Cohort I (2016) N = 35, and Cohort II (2016) N = 19. Responses of 0 and 1 were combined into one category. Columns do not sum to exactly 100% due to rounding.

serve very high-needs student populations. There were no differences between Cohort I and Cohort II students' perceptions of mastery-based instructional practices, and students' reported experiences of these approaches in spring 2016 were consistent with responses in spring 2015.

Teachers reported that some practices consistent with personalized learning were more common in 2016 than 2015. Overall, these responses are consistent with those from the first year of the study, but teachers reported emphasizing two practices— frequent regrouping and giving students opportunities to choose the instructional materials they use in class—slightly more in 2016 than in 2015. Teachers we interviewed confirmed that the most common way data were used to support personalization was through grouping students according to their needs. In 2016, Cohort II teachers reported emphasizing student choice and adapting course content to meet student needs to a slightly larger extent than Cohort I teachers.

Cohort II teachers were less likely to report obstacles to personalizing learning for students than Cohort I teachers. Although some teachers in both cohorts perceived a variety of factors to be obstacles to personalization (e.g., lack of curriculum flexibility, scheduling constraints, amount of time needed to prepare personalized lessons), in most cases Cohort II teachers were less likely to perceive these factors as major or minor obstacles than Cohort I teachers. In addition, Cohort I teachers were more likely to perceive these factors as obstacles in the second year of the school's operation (spring 2016) than in the first year (spring 2015), as shown in Figure 4.2. This pattern is similar to cohort differences in teachers' perceptions of obstacles to mastery, described above. The survey and interview data suggest several possible reasons for this pattern. One possibility is that the Cohort II schools learned valuable lessons from observing Cohort I schools and were therefore able to avoid certain pitfalls. Cohort I schools were staffed with less-experienced teachers, and

Designing Innovative High Schools
Implementation of the Opportunity by Design Initiative After Two Years

experience could have influenced teachers' perceptions of obstacles. Finally, Springpoint staff reported in interviews that the supports they provided to the Cohort II schools in their design year had improved over time, and this could partly account for this cross-cohort difference.

Cohort II teachers reported more teaching experience and perceived themselves to be better prepared for teaching in an ObD school than Cohort I teachers, but Cohort I teachers reported more-helpful supports. Cohort I teachers reported fewer years of teaching on average: 29 percent of Cohort II teachers had five or fewer years of teaching experience, compared with 57 percent of Cohort I teachers, as shown in Figure 4.3. Cohort II teachers were more likely to report that their teacher preparation program prepared them to teach in an ObD school to a large extent. Cohort II teachers' perceptions of their preparation exceeded those of Cohort I teachers in 2016 and in 2015. Another indicator of Cohort II teachers' readiness for teaching in ObD schools is the extent to which they chose to teach at their schools. A large majority of Cohort II teachers reported that fit with their interests and background affected their decision to take the job to a large or moderate extent, while one-fifth of Cohort I teachers reported that being placed in the school by the district (to any extent) influenced acceptance of the position.

One factor that could explain these patterns is that there was high teacher turnover in many of the Cohort I schools after the first year of operation. In interviews, some principals said it was challenging to recruit qualified candidates, and it is possible that a lack of experienced candidates may have led principals to hire less-experienced teachers. In addition, according to principals, teacher hiring rules in two of the Cohort I districts both restricted which teachers they could hire, and also required the schools to accept teachers placed there. One possible result of these conditions could be a staff in which fewer teachers were there by choice and were perhaps less interested in, or prepared to be, teaching in an innovative environment. A third possible explanation is the speed with which the design teams, which included the school leader, were assembled. Compared with Cohort I schools, the design teams were assembled and principals hired earlier in the design year in the Cohort II schools. The expanded time frame enabled Cohort II principals to begin hiring teachers earlier, which might have given them access to more-experienced candidates.

Cohort I teachers reported receiving more supports and finding them more helpful in their second year of operation (2015–2016) than in their first year. Specifically, Cohort I teachers reported receiving and finding helpful common planning time, a formal mentor or coach, opportunities to observe other teachers, and district PD.

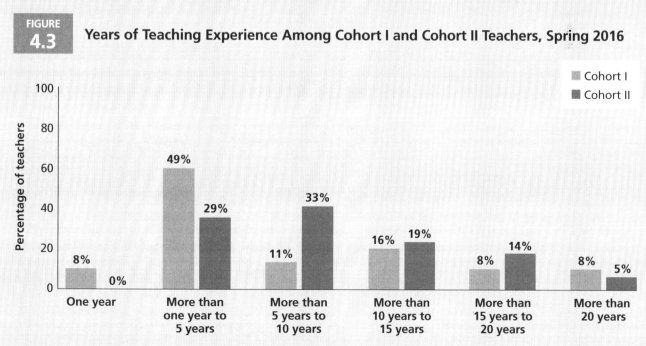

FIGURE 4.3 Years of Teaching Experience Among Cohort I and Cohort II Teachers, Spring 2016

NOTE: Survey question: "Including this school year (2015–2016), how many total years have you been teaching, regardless of location?" Responses were given in years in an open-ended text box and coded into ranges. Cohort I N = 37; Cohort II N = 21.

School Management and Operations

Cohort II teachers reported high levels of collegiality, collaboration, support for innovation, and effective management in their schools. Although 82 percent of teachers agreed or strongly agreed that teachers at their schools supported each other in their efforts to improve student learning, 52 percent of Cohort II teachers reported strong agreement with this statement, compared with 31 percent of Cohort I teachers. Cohort II teachers were more likely to strongly agree (56 percent) that their school promoted innovation and initiative among teachers and staff than Cohort I teachers (31 percent). Figure 4.4 shows that Cohort II teachers were more likely to agree that aspects of their schools' operations were managed effectively and efficiently than Cohort I teachers.

 FIGURE 4.4 **Cohort I and Cohort II Teachers' Agreement with Statements About School Operations, Spring 2016**

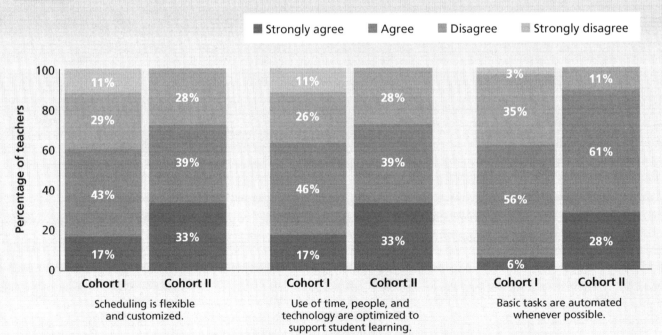

■ Strongly agree ■ Agree ■ Disagree ■ Strongly disagree

Percentage of teachers

Scheduling is flexible and customized.
- Cohort I: 11%, 29%, 43%, 17%
- Cohort II: 28%, 39%, 33%

Use of time, people, and technology are optimized to support student learning.
- Cohort I: 11%, 26%, 46%, 17%
- Cohort II: 28%, 39%, 33%

Basic tasks are automated whenever possible.
- Cohort I: 3%, 35%, 56%, 6%
- Cohort II: 11%, 61%, 28%

NOTE: Survey question: "Please rate your level of agreement with each of the [above] statements about your school." Response options were given on a 4-point scale ranging from "Strongly disagree" = 1 to "Strongly agree" = 4. Cohort I N = 34–35; Cohort II N = 18.

CHAPTER FIVE
District Context

Although the primary implementers of the ObD design principles are the teachers and school leaders who interact directly with students each day, the broader district, community, and state contexts in which schools operate inevitably influence implementation of school reforms. District conditions are especially salient for ObD because of the significant resources and structural conditions needed to support practices such as personalization. These conditions might facilitate smooth rollout and high-quality implementation of the design principles, or they might create barriers that hinder school staff from engaging in effective practices. This chapter summarizes overarching themes regarding implementation at the district level from the perspective of district and school leaders in both cohorts.

Districts gave ObD schools autonomy and flexibility in a variety of ways. Leaders in five of the six districts reported deliberate strategies designed to give the ObD schools greater autonomy and flexibility than other district schools. In four districts, the ObD schools had autonomy from the district in their hiring practices. In one of these districts, an intermediary organization worked with the ObD schools to design the hiring process. Intermediary leaders reported that their ability to design the hiring process and offer teachers leadership roles helped them to attract high-quality teachers to the school. In the districts without hiring autonomy, principals reported that they were limited to hiring teachers from within the district and that this made it difficult to find teachers invested in the ObD model. Leaders in one of these districts indicated that they were trying to change policy to allow the ObD schools to hire externally. ObD schools also had significant autonomy over their curricula, and staff members at all ten schools reported that teachers generally created their own curricula. In three districts, leaders specified that the ObD schools had the opportunity to attend district PD but were afforded flexibility in determining what would be most useful and relevant for their schools.

District support for curriculum design and implementation was uneven. One of the potential downsides to districts offering significant autonomy in the area of curriculum is that school-level staff might not always have the capacity (in terms of time and expertise) to find or create high-quality curriculum materials and implement them effectively. Although some teachers appreciated the opportunity to create or select their own curricula, many also raised questions about the quality of available materials, particularly online materials. Many teachers also expressed concerns about their own capacity to create curriculum aligned with the mastery and personalized learning principles.

Aside from autonomy, district leaders did not describe specific supports for helping the ObD schools to develop curricula. However, some ObD districts provided mastery specialists as a support to schools. Mastery specialists had expertise in developing and implementing mastery-based learning, and their role was to help teachers develop rubrics, align curriculum to standards, and research online curriculum and LMS options. Intermediary organizations in two of the districts offered targeted help for curriculum development in areas where available curricula were sparse, including for career and technical education and mastery-based curriculum for ELL. The need to devise curricula to meet individual student needs, and to identify or develop high-quality measures of mastery, was a key challenge faced by teachers in ObD schools.

Aligned district visions and systems have potential to support the spread of innovation. Leaders across all six districts described the ObD model as aligned to the district's vision. District staff said the broader goal was to scale innovative schools to better meet the needs of all students in their districts and to prepare them for college and career success. All districts hoped to learn from the implementation of the ObD schools, and they described different strategies intended to facilitate the spread of innovation. Three districts had mechanisms for school

> *"Even if they were only there for three hours, Springpoint is a group of people who can look at something in three hours and go, 'Oh yeah, this is . . . here's the thing.' And what's interesting is that when we compared notes on what we saw, we were in lockstep, which was wonderful."*
>
> **—COHORT I DISTRICT LEADER**

leaders to meet regularly as part of a network of other district leaders so they could share their experiences with innovative practices. In one of these districts, schools were recently re-organized from geographic networks into content-specific networks, and the ObD schools were put into a network that the district hoped would act as a "learning laboratory" for innovation. Another district created "design playbooks" that documented school- and system-level development as part of ObD implementation and intended to share them locally and nationally. This district utilized an internal Innovation Lab to share lessons about how teacher practice in innovative classrooms could lead to overall school improvement.

In addition to disseminating lessons learned from the ObD schools, leaders in some districts said they were working to align their systems to support the ObD principles. In one district, leaders reported that the ObD work spurred a change in their approach to teaching and learning, which led them to plan to redesign district technology systems and human capital strategies. In another district, leaders reported that they were working to revise the grading policy to better support mastery. Although we do not yet have direct evidence regarding the spread of innovation throughout the districts, these mechanisms for sharing innovative practices and capturing and disseminating learning have the potential to support the spread of innovation.

Intermediary organizations supplemented district support. In two districts, intermediary organizations supported the ObD schools. CCNY and Springpoint leaders suggested that these intermediaries brought expertise beyond what is typically found in districts and thus benefited the ObD schools. Comments from school and district leaders in these districts support the notion that intermediaries can extend district

capacity. Both intermediaries provided individualized support to the ObD schools for implementing their school-specific goals and the ObD design principles. One intermediary organization shared resources and connected ObD school leaders to other schools to learn about best practices for hiring after learning about the school's problems hiring teachers in 2015. In the other district, intermediary staff described their role as advocates for the ObD schools during the design process. Intermediary leaders provided extensive support to ObD principals during the design year and supported their interactions with the district. As mentioned earlier, these intermediaries also provided targeted support for curriculum development to the ObD schools in areas where curriculum resources were scarce.

Springpoint has extended district capacity in important ways. Regardless of whether they worked with an intermediary organization, all district and school leaders described positive and helpful support from Springpoint. Many district leaders described receiving unique and personalized support from Springpoint, suggesting that Springpoint's in-depth knowledge of each district's strengths and challenges helped make the partnership successful. In two districts, both of which experienced changes in leadership, Springpoint supported the district to continue ObD implementation even though the original district leaders were no longer involved. In one of these districts, leaders new to the ObD work reported that Springpoint provided an "honest narrative" of ObD implementation in Year One, which allowed them to better support the ObD schools in Year Two. In the other district, Springpoint extended district capacity for staff development. In this district, the mastery specialist reported a lack of training from the district and instead relied upon guidance from Springpoint to guide her work in the ObD schools. In the districts that did not experience leadership turnover, district staff suggested that continuity of leadership—in the district and in Springpoint—has been one important facilitator of the relationship. In three such districts, staff talked about how alignment between their district's vision and the ObD design principles facilitated accessing support from Springpoint. Several districts considered Springpoint a valuable partner in their work of supporting the ObD schools and praised Springpoint's ability to connect the districts with targeted resources and specific feedback on implementation.

CHAPTER SIX

Early Lessons for the Field

In this chapter, we summarize key strengths associated with ObD model implementation thus far, and we discuss some of the primary challenges that schools faced in the first one or two years of implementation. We identified two broad categories of challenges—those directly related to school design and others that are more related to the broader policy context in which the ObD schools operate; we discuss both in this chapter. We then present recommendations to promote high-quality implementation of ObD and other innovative models during the early years of school operation.

Summary of Strengths and Challenges

At this early stage in implementation, the ObD schools have demonstrated progress but also face numerous challenges. At all schools, staff and student reports suggest that implementation of key design principles (e.g., alignment of mission with school design, emphasis on mastery and personalized instructional approaches) is high across schools and improving over time and across cohorts. Across schools, student perceptions of school culture are positive and teachers' opinions of their PD experiences have improved over time. Also, Cohort II teachers reported more-extensive adoption of mastery-based and personalized instructional practices, and fewer obstacles to adopting such practices, than Cohort I teachers. District and school leaders reported that Springpoint support has been valuable and has helped spread best practices and align systems in a way that has the potential to facilitate the spread of innovation.

Implementation of these complex reforms is challenging, however, and there are limited examples of schools that integrate the ten design principles in the way the ObD schools aim to do. Therefore, the design and policy challenges faced by the ObD schools thus far suggest useful lessons for the field. Across schools, efforts to personalize instruction and implement mastery-based approaches were often inconsistent and limited by varying access to data, external pressure to advance students at a certain pace, and the significant time required to create instructional materials. Human capital challenges and lack of high-quality instructional materials exacerbated these challenges. Persistent teacher vacancies limited collaboration and strained teacher capacity, and principals reported difficulties finding and retaining qualified, experienced teachers. High-quality instructional materials were not readily available, and although teachers reported that they had the autonomy to create their own materials, they struggled to find the time to do so and received limited district support. Amid these challenges, most schools had yet to develop clear systems for data-driven improvement, instead responding to feedback and addressing issues as they arose.

Implementation Strengths

Implementation of key design principles is reportedly high and is improving with time within and across cohorts. Our data suggest that implementation of the mastery, personalization, and PYD design principles was high across schools, years, and cohorts. Further, implementation of key principles (i.e., mission and culture, personalization, and mastery) appeared to improve from Year One to Year Two. A comparison of implementation in Cohort I schools from the first to second year of implementation suggests that those schools improved in several areas as they refined their school structures and systems. In particular, the alignment between school mission and school model improved, as did teachers' opinions of the clarity of the mission. In Year Two, interviewed school staff in both cohorts described missions that were more clearly defined, better aligned with the documented mission, and more consistent with the design principles than in Year One.

Similarly, a comparison of the first year of implementation for Cohort I (2014–2015) and Cohort II (2015–2016) schools provides evidence that implementation of personalized and mastery-based approaches often occurred with greater intensity and fewer obstacles in the Cohort II schools; we discuss this in more detail later in this chapter. Cohort II teachers reported that they had more teaching experience and that they were more prepared to teach in ObD schools. They also expressed slightly more-positive opinions about their school data systems and reported more-frequent receipt of student mastery data than did Cohort I teachers in Year Two.

There are at least three possible explanations for the observed improvement in implementation over time. One possibility is that the Cohort II schools had opportunities to incorporate lessons learned from Cohort I schools (e.g., through Springpoint study tours) into their school design and implementation plans.

Another is that Springpoint refined its approach to supporting schools over time (e.g., spending more time working in small groups, providing one-on-one coaching, analyzing artifacts, and providing connections to external experts) and in Year Two was likely able to support schools more effectively than in Year One. A third is that the schools may have improved their ability to use data to quickly identify problems and implement solutions. We cannot say with confidence that these differences are the result of superior implementation on the part of the Cohort II schools; they could be a result of differences in teaching experience, teachers' perceived preparation to teach in an innovative school, or other factors.

Springpoint provided key supports to ObD districts and schools. As a technical assistance and support organization, Springpoint's role was to support the ObD schools through the design process and the early years of implementation. Principals reported that support from Springpoint was particularly valuable, and these perceptions have improved over time. District leaders also praised Springpoint's support and indicated that it was particularly helpful for aligning district visions, systems, and policies to support ObD and facilitate innovation. Several district leaders mentioned that support from Springpoint was a way to extend district capacity and smooth challenges that were the result of leadership turnover, lack of district experience with PD to support these innovative approaches, and resource constraints. District and school leaders both mentioned ObD school walkthroughs and study tours as particularly helpful, and school leaders found the connections to consultants to be valuable. These positive reports suggest that the Springpoint approach of providing technical assistance and support has the potential to be a useful model for supporting similar large-scale reform efforts within and across districts.

Key Design Challenges

Lack of high-quality curriculum materials and projects limited some aspects of mastery-based and personalized instruction. The recent transition to new standards in many states, combined with the difficulty of finding instructional materials to support high levels of personalization in the ObD schools, have placed heavy demands on many teachers to select or create a curriculum that meets student needs. Most of the ObD schools relied on teacher-created or teacher-selected materials to some extent, largely because district-provided curriculum materials tended to be limited and not well aligned with the needs of the school, and were not well-suited to personalization. However, although many teachers valued having the autonomy to design or select materials, a lack of time to develop personalized materials was described by teachers and school leaders as a key challenge to implementing personalized and mastery-based learning for all students, and many teachers raised questions about the quality of available materials, particularly online materials. The ObD districts did not seem to provide specific supports for helping teachers develop or identify curriculum materials suitable for personalized and mastery-based environments, other than providing teachers with the autonomy to select or develop their own materials.

In these early years of operation, we found that the lack of existing materials limited the extent to which students could progress at their own pace—students could only advance as far as the existing materials would allow. Similarly, many teachers said that grouping students for projects also limited the extent to which students could work at their own pace because projects usually require some amount of instruction to ensure students have a similar understanding of the topic and content of the project. When teaching with projects, teachers felt the need to move slower students along so that they could introduce the relevant content even if those students had not yet mastered what they were currently working on.

Staffing issues and inconsistent access to data also limited implementation of high-quality mastery-based and personalized instructional approaches. One aim of personalized and mastery-based instructional approaches is to provide consistently high-quality instruction for all students. We found that the ObD schools were still working toward this aim and identified several challenges. In some schools, inadequate staffing stretched the capacity of existing staff (e.g., teachers were obliged to give up their planning periods to cover classes, thus further reducing the time available to create materials and personalize lessons), and, in a few schools, key positions (e.g., mathematics) were vacant due to lack of qualified staff. Also, teachers' access to data to support mastery-based instruction varied, and likely made it more difficult for teachers to implement mastery-based and personalized approaches. Teachers reported receiving various types of achievement data at least monthly, but many teachers expressed a need for more or better data to gauge student progress toward mastery.

Variation in methods for assessing mastery and external pressure to advance students at a certain pace made it challenging to maintain universally high expectations for students. At this early stage in implementation, tasks used to assess mastery across the ObD schools varied in terms of scope and quality, and staff expressed a need for improving the consistency and rigor of tasks assessed for mastery. In three districts, tasks assessed for mastery were generally described by teachers as summative performance tasks or projects that took place after students had spent some time learning content or practicing skills. In the other three districts, teachers described using a variety of assessment types to determine mastery, ranging from quick online quizzes and worksheets to larger projects. This variety of methods seemed to contribute to inconsistent or low expectations for mastery, with the result that the criteria for mastery did not always set a high bar for student work (e.g., in one school the standard for mastery was mastering 65 percent of the standards at a Level 3 or greater), and scoring guidelines were not always consistently applied (e.g., a score of 2 on the rubric could mean different things for different teachers, and for different students). Some principals noted that some staff assigned mastery tasks that did not appear to be rigorous (e.g., worksheets, short quizzes) or inconsistently applied the mastery standard (i.e., expected higher-level work from some students, but not from others). Even in the three schools where teachers did not explicitly mention inconsistent expectations for rigor and mastery, this inconsistency was evident in teachers' discussions.

In addition, although most teachers reported extensive use of specific mastery-based practices, none of the ObD schools had yet developed a system for student advancement that was wholly mastery-based—teacher and principal discretion was a factor in student advancement decisions. Many teachers said they felt pressure to move at a set pace through the curriculum, thus limiting students' ability to work at their own pace to master the material. Sources of this pressure varied from a need to prepare students for accountability assessments, to limited teacher capacity to differentiate pace for all students, to poor student attendance and limited work completion. Some principals reported feeling external pressure to ensure that students graduated within the expected four years, even if the data suggested additional time was warranted.

Key Policy Challenges

Schools found it challenging to hire and retain teachers and leaders whose preparation and interests were aligned with ObD models.
All principals had difficulty recruiting and hiring qualified candidates who were a good fit for the school model and were experienced in mastery-based and personalized learning practices, particularly in mathematics, science, and engineering, regardless of whether they were exempt from district hiring practices. According to principals in all districts, it was difficult to find qualified applicants, and principals in the four districts that lacked hiring flexibility reported particular trouble recruiting teachers from within their districts who had relevant experience and were invested in the ObD model. Teacher retention was mentioned as a challenge by all principals and seemed to be a particular problem in five schools, one of which, a Cohort I school, had not had a mathematics teacher since opening in 2014. Teacher vacancies strained staff capacity and limited teachers' ability to fully implement mastery-based and personalized approaches. In the three schools that experienced principal turnover, teachers described difficulties resulting from these leadership transitions as contributing to teacher turnover.

Teacher experience and perceptions of preparation for teaching in an ObD school varied. Cohort II teachers reported more years of teaching experience than Cohort I teachers and were more likely to report that

their teacher preparation program had prepared them to teach in an ObD school. One factor that could explain this pattern is that there was high teacher turnover in many of the Cohort I schools after the first year of operation. According to principals, there was a lack of qualified applicants, which may have led these schools to hire less-experienced teachers. Also, according to principals, teacher hiring rules in two Cohort I districts restricted which teachers they could hire, resulting in school staffs with fewer teachers prepared or willing to teach in an innovative environment. These persistent challenges suggest that specialized support for staffing (e.g., consultant services to recruit qualified teachers, resources to train less-experienced staff), in addition to autonomy and flexibility from district hiring practices, may be necessary to support implementation of ObD design principles.

Autonomy and opportunities to provide feedback are necessary conditions for innovation and change, but other supports are required. Most teachers reported high levels of autonomy and the ability to provide input regarding the school model, and these conditions seemed to support innovation. Teachers reportedly valued the autonomy to create their own curriculum materials, design courses, and make key instructional decisions, and several teachers mentioned, in interviews, that this autonomy and

the opportunity to innovate were reasons they took the position at the school. Similarly, the ability to provide input on the school model, address issues, and implement changes was reported, and valued, by teachers at most schools. However, teachers reported struggling to develop high-quality curriculum materials, citing lack of time, few good examples, and limited PD as barriers. Although staff at all schools said they had the ability to make changes in response to feedback, most schools seemed to struggle with ensuring that key aspects of the school model supported the mission and were regularly monitored to ensure effective implementation and did not have clear mechanisms in place to monitor alignment.

There is also evidence that students needed supports to adjust to the autonomy afforded them in these mastery-based systems. In particular, in schools that offered flexible deadlines designed to provide students with multiple opportunities to revise and master the material, teachers reported that an unintended consequence of this approach was that students often waited to turn in assignments until right before grades were due. Taken together, these data suggest that additional supports, such as resources to develop high-quality curriculum materials or processes for monitoring change, are necessary for innovation and change for students as well as teachers.

Recommendations for Supporting Continued Implementation of ObD Models

In this final section, we offer some preliminary recommendations for supporting implementation of innovative school designs, particularly during the early years. These recommendations are relevant to districts and intermediary organizations that work directly with schools, but they are also intended to inform the work of funders and technical assistance providers who need to decide how to allocate resources and supports, including PD. In some cases, state education agencies might also play an important role, particularly in states that have adopted new standards and that are developing resources to promote standards-aligned instruction.

Provide teachers with support and assistance to develop and select curriculum materials. ObD teachers reported spending significant time and effort on creating, finding, and adapting curriculum resources. This is consistent with research findings nationally, in large part in response to CCSS implementation. While many ObD teachers enjoyed developing their own curriculum materials and felt that it gave them an opportunity to use their professional knowledge and training in creative ways, many reported that it was time-consuming to develop their own materials and difficult to locate high-quality materials. Largely because of the time required to develop original curriculum materials, teacher-created materials were not always personalized to students' individual needs. State, district, intermediary organization, and school leaders could consider working with teachers to set expectations for time spent developing materials and provide additional support to teachers in the form of external experts (e.g., consultants, dedicated staff), common planning time, or resources (e.g., funding, staff time) to research and vet ready-made materials.

Ensure that teachers have access to high-quality data to implement mastery-based and personalized approaches and the support to use them effectively. Varied access to high-quality data suitable for informing mastery-based and personalized approaches was one inhibitor to teachers' ability to implement such approaches for all students. School and district leaders could consider talking with teachers and experts to discover what data would be most useful for supporting personalized and mastery-based approaches, and how frequently and in what formats teachers would like to receive such data. Ideally, high-quality data should be aligned with the curriculum, frequently updated, and easily accessible. Data on students' academic progress are essential, but data on other outcomes, such as socioemotional competencies, would be valuable for ObD schools, particularly given the models' focus on promoting PYD. Additional PD to support data use could also be valuable, particularly for those teachers who indicated that they had plenty of data but were not sure how to make sense of it or use it for instructional decisionmaking.

Develop systems and processes to ensure that all students receive high-quality instruction and are held to high expectations. We found variety in the complexity of tasks used to assess mastery, the way mastery-based grading systems were applied, and the quality of teacher-developed curriculum materials. The diversity of curriculum and instructional materials available, combined with the lack of consistent curriculum supports, the need to personalize instruction, and the variation in how mastery-based systems were used, made it challenging for school leaders to monitor instruction and ensure that instructional quality and expectations are high for all students.

District leaders could consider providing resources (e.g., time, consultant services, frameworks, or example materials) to support school leaders and teachers to develop systems and processes to review curriculum materials, compare assessments of student work, and provide ongoing professional development with the goal of creating mastery-based systems that are consistently applied and hold all students to high expectations. District and school leaders could consider working with teachers and external experts to find systems that integrate personalized instruction with high-quality data to monitor mastery, providing teachers with more training to use them, and continuously reviewing student progress to identify students who are not on a trajectory that will lead to mastery at grade level or higher. Leaders could also increase networking opportunities for teachers within and across ObD schools so they can share strategies for promoting high expectations. School leaders could consider staffing approaches, such as team-teaching, using two adults in the classroom, or pairing less-experienced and more-experienced teachers, which could help facilitate consistently high-quality instruction and high expectations for students.

Offer specialized support for recruiting, hiring, and retention, while encouraging autonomy and flexibility in district policies. A human capital strategy that includes consistent, high-quality systems for sourcing and selecting teachers and staff, and is aligned with the school model and priorities, is a key ObD design principle and an important component of successful implementation of other design principles. The challenges related to staff recruitment, hiring, and retention, such as teacher hiring rules in some districts, and recruiting qualified candidates who were a good fit, especially in hard-to-staff subjects such as mathematics and engineering, suggest that supports specifically designed to help school leaders recruit, hire, and retain teachers are needed. In particular, district leaders might consider relaxing hiring policies, working with teachers' unions to develop policies that support school autonomy in hiring, and providing the ObD schools (and other innovative schools) with the autonomy and other supports to successfully recruit, hire, and retain the staff of their choosing. Districts might also consider supporting innovative schools to design recruiting strategies to specifically target teachers interested in and qualified to be teaching in an innovative environment.

Consider ways to offer principals continued support beyond the first two years of implementation as they refine their models and hire new staff. We know reforms take a long time to get right, and this one is particularly complex. In the spirit of continuous improvement, the ObD schools are continuing to refine their models and train new staff. Principals valued many of the supports they received during the first two years—particularly support from Springpoint—and some mechanism for continuing to provide these supports could help the schools build on the work they have done and sustain improvement in the models over time. It may be particularly important to provide resources and support to help principals manage their school operations efficiently and develop clear processes for data-driven continuous improvement, since this is an area in which most schools have not yet developed such processes. This support could take a variety of forms based on schools' needs and contexts, and could include additional support from Springpoint in the form of study tours or connections to consultants, as well as targeted support from the districts. Our data suggest that the Cohort I schools are still working to refine their models, particularly their mastery systems, and they could benefit from continued support in this area, especially if they experienced leadership turnover. In addition, our data suggest that the Cohort II schools reported fewer challenges than did the Cohort I schools in their first year, and Springpoint, in its role as connector and convener of ObD schools, could help current and future schools incorporate lessons learned during the early years of implementation.

APPENDIX: Methods

The analyses of implementation of the ObD models were designed to examine the features of each school's model, the ways that educators were implementing those features thus far (over either one or two years), and the challenges and facilitators associated with implementation. The analyses produced information that can be aggregated across schools and districts while also being sensitive to the unique features of each school's approach. We describe each of our implementation data-collection approaches below. Numbers of interview and focus group participants are summarized in Table A.1; survey response rates are summarized in Table A.2.

Annual Fall Interviews with District, Springpoint, and CCNY Staff

We conducted one-hour telephone interviews with key staff at CCNY, Springpoint, each ObD district, and intermediary organizations in two districts between fall 2015 and winter 2016, as shown in Table A.1. Interviewers followed semistructured interview protocols to balance consistency in the questions asked and ensure coverage of important content while also allowing for respondents to elaborate or offer unsolicited input. The interviews helped us

gather information about district context, the ways in which the district supported the ObD schools, future plans for implementation, challenges, and successes. We interviewed five district staff members, two Springpoint staff members, two CCNY staff members, and three staff members across the two intermediary organizations.

Annual Spring School Visits

We conducted two-day, in-person visits at each ObD school in May 2016. The purpose of the site visits was to gather in-depth information about implementation of the school model and instructional practices and to solicit student and parent perspectives. During each visit, we interviewed the school principal and, if applicable, another school leader in a position to provide insight on implementation of the design principles. At each school, we selected four teachers to participate in 45-minute interviews. If no second school leader was available, we interviewed a fifth teacher. Two teachers participated in artifact-based interviews, intended to capture evidence regarding some important aspects of instructional practice. Teachers were asked to bring class assignments, assessment criteria or rubrics, and examples of student work to the artifact interviews. Two to three teachers participated in school design interviews focused on asking teachers to describe aspects of the school design along with perceived challenges and facilitators. Total teaching staff sizes in these schools ranged from ten to 15. We also conducted one-hour focus groups with six to eight students, one-hour focus groups with four to eight parents in four schools, and ten- to 15-minute observations of four to six classrooms where mathematics or English language arts (ELA) instruction was taking place. Across schools, we interviewed 13 school leaders and 46 teachers; conducted ten student focus groups with a total of 65 students and four parent focus groups with a total of 14 parents; observed 42 classrooms; and collected and reviewed 30 artifacts, as shown in Table A.1.

We selected teachers to ensure variability in years of teaching experience, subjects taught, and grade level, if applicable. A school administrator selected students for the focus group so that the group would include students with a mix of ages, interests, and

Table A.1. Number of Interview Participants and Focus Groups, 2015–2016

Data-Collection Method	Source	N
Interviews	CCNY and Springpoint staff	4
	District and intermediary leaders	8
	School leaders	13[a]
	Teachers	46
Focus groups[b]	Students	10
	Parents	4
Observations	Classroom	42
Artifacts	Assignments, assessment reports	30

[a] The school leader interview N is 13 because we requested permission to interview up to two leaders in each school. We interviewed all ten principals, and in three schools we also interviewed a second school leader (i.e., a mastery specialist, a design fellow, and a campus coordinator).

[b] Focus group N represents the number of groups, not the number of participants. Across schools, 65 students and 14 parents participated in focus groups. Only four schools provided permission to conduct parent focus groups.

learning levels, as well as students of both genders. We used semistructured interview and focus group protocols to promote consistency in the questions asked across schools and to ensure coverage of important content while also allowing for respondents to elaborate or offer unsolicited input. The classroom observation protocol was open-ended to allow observers to capture the diversity of instructional approaches and classroom arrangements. The protocol captured classroom conditions such as student-to-adult ratios, presence of technology, type and content of instruction, teacher and student interactions, and the nature of student groupings.

Annual Spring Principal and Teacher Surveys

Principals and teachers of core academic content areas (i.e., mathematics, ELA, and science) were invited to participate in web-based surveys in spring 2016. The surveys gathered systematic information about principals' and teachers' perceptions about various aspects of the models, including professional training and support, access to resources, the quality of instructional and curriculum materials, use of different models of classroom instruction, use of technology in the classroom, use of data to assess student progress, and obstacles to implementation. The principal survey took approximately ten minutes to complete; the teacher survey took approximately 30 minutes to complete. Although many of the survey items were developed specifically for this study, several were adapted from other RAND surveys (including those used in Pane et al., 2015) or from surveys developed

by the University of Chicago Consortium on School Research.

Teacher survey response rates ranged from 60 percent to 100 percent across schools, with an overall response rate of 81 percent. In total, 75 teachers were surveyed, and 61 responded.

We administered the principal survey to all principals with the exception of one school where the principal had resigned. At that school, the district's mastery specialist, who was the acting principal, responded to the survey. All selected respondents (ten out of ten) completed the survey. School-level survey and IRQ response rates are shown in Table A.2.

Annual Fall and Spring IRQs

Teachers of core academic content areas (i.e., mathematics, ELA, and science) were invited to participate in web-based IRQs—brief, online surveys that included questions about daily instructional practices and the factors that influenced their teaching on a particular day. Teachers in their first year of teaching at an ObD school were exempt from participating in the fall IRQs, but they were invited to participate in the spring. We administered the IRQs over two ten-day periods in 2015–2016, once in the fall and once in the spring, for a total of 20 IRQs per teacher. In the fall, the IRQs were distributed to a sample of 35 teachers, and 29 teachers completed at least one IRQ in which they indicated that they had provided instruction that day, for a response rate of 83 percent. In the spring, the IRQs were distributed to

Table A.2. Survey and IRQ Response Rates, by School, 2015–2016

Cohort	School	Teacher Survey N	Teacher Survey Response Rate (%)	Fall IRQ N	Fall IRQ Response Rate (%)	Spring IRQ N	Spring IRQ Response Rate (%)	Fall Student Survey N	Fall Student Survey Response Rate (%)	Spring Student Survey N	Spring Student Survey Response Rate (%)
I	A	9	75	5	63	7	58	150	82	150	87
	B	11	100	7	100	11	100	138	95	141	87
	C	7	78	4	100	9	100	137	98	152	94
	D	5	63	7	88	3	38	186	95	128	70
	E	6	86	6	75	6	86	142	94	118	86
II	F	4	80	—	—	4	80	88	90	82	88
	G	4	80	—	—	3	60	92	96	89	100
	H	3	60	—	—	3	60	91	100	85	99
	I	5	83	—	—	7	100	67	96	63	100
	J	7	100	—	—	6	100	70	95	62	91
Total		61	81	29	83	59	79	1,161	93	1,070	88

NOTES: IRQ response rates reported are for teachers who completed at least one IRQ. Student survey response rates reported are among students with consent. Cohort II schools did not participate in the fall IRQs because they were in their first year of operation.

a sample of 75 teachers, and 59 teachers completed at least one IRQ in which they indicated that they had provided instruction that day, for a response rate of 79 percent, as shown in Table A.2.

The number of IRQs completed varied by teacher; missing IRQs were due either to a response of "I did not provide instruction today" or to noncompletion. Each day, teachers answered a series of questions while focusing on their interactions with one student during the first 45 minutes of mathematics or ELA instruction. Teachers were asked to focus on a different student each day that they completed the IRQ. The rationale for asking teachers to focus on a single student rather than the entire class is that the instruction offered, and the nature of the student-teacher interactions, can vary across students. This variability is particularly likely to occur in environments that use personalized instructional strategies. In this report, IRQ data are used to triangulate with other data sources and are not reported separately.

Annual Fall and Spring Student Surveys

Students were invited to participate in a brief (20-to-30-minute) online survey in fall 2015 and in spring 2016. The fall survey included questions about study habits, attitudes toward learning, and goals for high school and beyond. The spring survey included the questions asked in the fall along with additional questions about students' perceptions of their school and classroom environments. We offered the survey in English, Spanish, French, Arabic, and written Chinese to all students after consulting with district staff about students' language needs. Fall response rates among students with consent ranged from 82 percent to 100 percent,[1] with an overall response rate of 93 percent. In total, 1,242 students were eligible to participate, and 1,161 students participated. Numbers of eligible students in each school ranged from 67 to 186. Spring response rates among students with consent ranged from 70 percent to 100 percent, with an overall response rate of 88 percent. In total, 1,218 students were eligible to participate, and 1,070 students participated, as shown in Table A.2. Numbers of eligible students in each school ranged from 62 to 152.

---

[1] In most schools, we were able to obtain passive consent from parents to allow their children to participate and therefore had consent from most students (one to four students per school opted out of the survey). One school required active parental consent; therefore, we had consent from fewer students (70 percent of students consented in the fall and 83 percent in the spring).

As with the teacher surveys, we developed many of the items specifically for this study, but the surveys also included original or modified versions of items from the Chicago Consortium's surveys; the High School Survey of Student Engagement, developed by the Center for Evaluation and Education Policy at Indiana University; and the RAND survey of student perceptions of personalized learning practices (Pane et al., 2015).

Annual Collection of Artifacts

We asked CCNY, Springpoint, district, and school interview participants to provide us with artifacts relevant to understanding ObD implementation. Examples of such artifacts included design documents such as work plans, school handbooks or competency maps, instructional materials such as rubrics or lesson plans, and other items, such as materials from PD sessions. We reviewed these documents to inform our understanding of the school designs and contexts.

Analytic Method

We analyzed the qualitative data using Dedoose software, which allowed us to code for common themes across data-collection sites and across sources (e.g., teachers, district administrators), maintaining a database of coded data that will grow as additional years of data are added to the study. The analysis of the interview and focus group data proceeded in several steps. First, interview notes were compared with the audio recording and cleaned to serve as a near-transcript of the conversation. The cleaned interview notes were then loaded into Dedoose and coded using a thematic codebook developed by the evaluation team to align with the ten design principles. Once the thematic coding was complete, we conducted a second round of coding, analyzing the data according to questions of interest (e.g., to what extent are schools implementing mastery-based progression?). In this stage, we used an inductive coding process (i.e., codes were derived from the data rather than from a structured codebook) to develop responses to the questions of interest. We engaged in member checking as appropriate to ensure data accuracy. Finally, we summarized implementation of each design principle across schools. We also summarized district, CCNY, and Springpoint perspectives on implementation.

We analyzed the quantitative data from the surveys and IRQs using statistical software (SAS and STATA). We conducted exploratory factor analyses for the student and teacher surveys to assess the appropriateness of combining individual items into multi-item scales.[2]

The IRQ was designed to provide evidence regarding the frequency with which teachers use particular practices and how that use varies. As discussed above, the IRQ data included information on multiple lessons per teacher. This feature of the IRQ data enables us to examine how instruction varies across lessons for an individual teacher, as well as to estimate the amount of variation in responses due to differences across teachers within the same school and to differences across schools. For IRQ items that were not dichotomous (i.e., those with more than two possible responses), we estimated the proportion of variance within teachers (that is, across lessons for the same teacher), between teachers, and between schools. For dichotomous items, we were able to decompose the variance into only two sources: between schools and within schools, since the latter variance component includes both the between-teacher variance and the within-teacher variance.

Limitations

The implementation data are drawn from a variety of sources and provide a rich picture of ObD model implementation. At the same time, readers should keep in mind the limitations of the data sources. In particular, the survey and interview data rely on the self-reports of stakeholders who voluntarily participated. We have no independent means of verifying the accuracy of their responses. Where response rates are lower, particularly for the teacher survey and IRQs in some schools, responses may not accurately represent the perceptions of the whole stakeholder group, limiting generalizability. Moreover, although the interview data are crucial for providing richness and context, the numbers of interview participants are small in many cases, and the teachers and students who participated in the interviews and focus groups are not representative samples of the full populations of teachers and students in the ObD schools. The comparisons of teacher survey responses across cohorts are limited by the small number of teachers in Cohort II schools and by the fact that the teachers in the two cohorts differ in some background characteristics (e.g., higher teaching experience levels among Cohort II teachers). The teacher survey sample size for Cohort I was 38 and for Cohort II was 23. Finally, without a national comparison group, we also have no way to determine whether the practices, facilitators, and challenges reported by ObD staff and students were substantively different from those used and experienced by educators and students nationally.

---

[2] We did not conduct exploratory factor analysis on the principal survey because of the small sample size. However, many of the items on these surveys were drawn from other surveys that had been subjected to exploratory factor analysis.

References

American College Testing for Youth, "Principles of Youth Development," web page, 2017. As of February 2, 2017: http://www.actforyouth.net/youth_development/development/

Are They Really Ready to Work? Employers' Perspectives on the Basic Knowledge and Applied Skills of New Entrants to the 21st Century U.S. Workforce, New York: The Conference Board, Partnership for 21st Century Skills, Corporate Voices for Working Families, and Society for Human Resource Management, 2006.

Bloom, Howard S., and Rebecca Unterman, *Sustained Progress: New Findings About the Effectiveness and Operation of Small Public High Schools of Choice in New York City*, New York: MDRC, 2013.

Carnegie Corporation of New York, *Opportunity by Design: New High School Models for Student Success*, New York, 2013.

———, email communication to the RAND project team about the purpose of the ObD Initiative and definitions of key terms, January 31, 2017.

CCNY—*See* Carnegie Corporation of New York.

Coburn, Cynthia E., and Erica O. Turner, "The Practice of Data Use: An Introduction," *American Journal of Education*, Vol. 118, No. 2, February 2012, pp. 99–111.

Hamilton, Laura, Richard Halverson, Sharnell S. Jackson, Ellen Mandinach, Jonathan A. Supovitz, Jeffrey C. Wayman, Cassandra Pickens, Emma Sama Martin, and Jennifer L. Steele, *Using Student Achievement Data to Support Instructional Decision Making*, Washington, D.C.: U.S. Department of Education, 2009. https://www.rand.org/pubs/external_publications/EP20090929.html

Kaufman, Julia H., Lindsey E. Thompson, and V. Darleen Opfer, *Creating a Coherent System to Support Instruction Aligned with State Standards: Promising Practices of the Louisiana Department of Education,* Santa Monica, Calif.: RAND Corporation, RR-1613-HCT, 2016. As of December 14, 2016: http://www.rand.org/pubs/research_reports/RR1613.html

Kemple, James J., and Cynthia Willner, *Career Academies: Long-Term Impacts on Labor Market Outcomes, Educational Attainment, and Transitions to Adulthood*, New York: MDRC, 2008.

Lake, Robin, Paul T. Hill, and Tricia Maas, *Next Generation School Districts: What Capacities Do Districts Need to Create and Sustain Schools That Are Ready to Deliver on Common Core?* Seattle, Wash.: Center on Reinventing Public Education, 2015.

Lewis, Matthew W., Rick Eden, Chandra Garber, Mollie Rudnick, Lucrecia Santibañez, and Tiffany Tsai, *Equity in Competency Education: Realizing the Potential, Overcoming the Obstacles*, Boston, Mass.: Jobs for the Future, 2014. https://www.rand.org/pubs/external_publications/EP66203.html

Long, Mark C., Dylan Conger, and Patrice Iatarola, "Effects of High School Course-Taking on Secondary and Postsecondary Success," *American Educational Research Journal*, Vol. 49, No. 2, April 2012, pp. 285–322.

NAEP—*See* National Assessment of Educational Progress.

Nagaoka, Jenny, Camille A. Farrington, Stacy B. Ehrlich, and Ryan D. Heath, *Foundations for Young Adult Success: A Developmental Framework*, Chicago, Ill.: Consortium for Chicago School Research, 2015.

National Assessment of Educational Progress, "The Nation's Report Card," web page, undated. As of December 13, 2016: http://www.nationsreportcard.gov/

National Center for Education Statistics, "Public High School Graduation Rates," web page, 2016. As of December 13, 2016: http://nces.ed.gov/programs/coe/indicator_coi.asp

NCES—*See* National Center for Education Statistics.

Pane, John F., Elizabeth D. Steiner, Matthew D. Baird, and Laura S. Hamilton, *Continued Progress: Promising Evidence on Personalized Learning*, Santa Monica, Calif.: RAND Corporation, RR-1365-BMGF, 2015. As of December 13, 2016: http://www.rand.org/pubs/research_reports/RR1365.html

Pellegrino, James W., and Margaret L. Hilton, *Education for Life and Work: Developing Transferable Knowledge and Skills in the 21st Century*, Washington, D.C.: National Academies Press, 2013.

Quint, Janet, *Meeting Five Critical Challenges of High School Reform: Lessons from Three Reform Models*, New York: MDRC, 2006.

reDesign, "The Mastery Learning Resource Bank," web page, 2017. As of February 2, 2017: http://www.redesignu.org/design-lab/mastery-learning/resource-bank

Scott-Clayton, Judith, and Olga Rodriguez, "Development, Discouragement, or Diversion? New Evidence of the Effects of College Remediation Policy," *Education Finance and Policy*, Vol. 10, No. 1, Winter 2015, pp. 4–45.

Soland, Jim, Laura S. Hamilton, and Brian M. Stecher, *Measuring 21st-Century Competencies: Guidance for Educators*, New York: Asia Society, 2013. https://www.rand.org/pubs/external_publications/EP50463.html

Springpoint Schools, *How Students Thrive: Positive Youth Development in Practice*, New York, February 21, 2017.

Sturgis, Chris, *Implementing Competency Education in K–12 Systems: Insights from Local Leaders*, Competency Works Issue Brief, Vienna, Va.: International Association for K–12 Online Learning, 2015.

U.S. Department of Education, *Using Evidence to Create Next Generation High Schools*, Washington, D.C.: Office of Planning, Evaluation and Policy Development, Policy and Program Studies Service, 2016.